HAUS CURIOSITIES

Fiction, Fact and Future

About the Author

James Elles was a British Conservative Member of the European Parliament from 1984 to 2014. He is the Co-founder of the European Internet Forum and the Founder and Chairman of the Transatlantic Policy Network. He is also the Honorary President of the European Strategic and Policy Analysis System (ESPAS).

James Elles

FICTION, FACT AND FUTURE

An Insight into EU Democracy

HAUS
CURIOSITIES

First published by Haus Publishing in 2019
4 Cinnamon Row
London SW11 3TW
www.hauspublishing.com

A CIP catalogue record for this book is
available from the British Library

Print ISBN: 978-1-912208-04-3
Ebook ISBN: 978-1-912208-03-6

Typeset in Garamond by MacGuru Ltd

Printed in Czech Republic

Contents

Preface

For more than 40 years, I have experienced an invigorating journey working within European Union (EU) institutions, principally as a Member of the European Parliament (MEP) representing electors in the Thames Valley, in the South East region of the UK, for a continuous period of 30 years. During this time, nothing has diminished my profound belief that strengthening the capacity for the EU to act on behalf of its citizens is the right course to take. Along the way, I have participated in, or seen at close quarters, many of the defining moments of the era. The EU has changed beyond all recognition, from being a community of nine countries with limited powers at its disposal to accommodating 28 member countries and 23 languages, with substantive powers giving it a global reach.

It is beyond the scope of this book to recount all my experiences or give my reflections on many of the key issues now under debate. But what I hope to do is to draw the attention of a young generation and show them the critical importance of the EU, which is so little understood in the UK – not least among our political leaders and commentators.

What this book seeks to illustrate is that there have been major changes to the way of life in our country over the past 45 years, through which we have helped create a remarkable organisation, enabling independent democratic European countries to find ways to resolve their differences together. They have done this not by being entirely nationalistic in their approach, but by realising that through sharing a limited degree of sovereignty they can increase the effectiveness of all of the EU's members to meet the major challenges ahead.

Unpredictability is a key factor in the world today. Though many trends can be identified to show how our societies are adapting at a revolutionary speed to new technologies – with connectivity and digital transformation affecting our environments – in contrast, British political attitudes have been moving at a snail's pace in terms of adjusting to changes in European institutions. The story of Britain's membership of the EU provides a cautionary tale of how not to make a success of the venture.

I hope that the insight arising from this book, underlining the vital importance of the EU to the stability and prosperity of our environment, will give hope to those who may shortly no longer be EU citizens, so that they are empowered to act and avert what could be a real tragedy for the UK.

Acknowledgements

The subject of this book is a story which has no end – the evolving nature of Britain's relationship with the EU as they both adjust to accelerating global change. As the title implies, it provides personal insight based on experiences I have had of the adjustments which have so far taken place, and explores what potentially lies for us in the decade ahead.

I am indebted firstly to Haus Publishing for giving me the exceptional opportunity at this historic moment to publish these reflections. Secondly, to those many colleagues and friends who have given me ideas which are freely expressed in the text. Lastly, but not least, to my family and in particular my wife Caroline who has been so supportive and inspirational.

> GERALD: I suppose society is wonderfully delightful!
> LORD ILLINGWORTH: To be in it is merely a bore, but to be out of it simply a tragedy.
>
> – Oscar Wilde, *A Woman of No Importance*

1

Fiction

Thanks to the votes cast by the British people in the referendum on 23rd June 2016, the UK decided to leave the EU. Looking back over the period of membership, there have been many times, not least since the referendum, when it has been legitimate to ask whether we as a country really ever understood what our commitments to EU membership were. As we shall see, many politicians were (and still are) seemingly totally unaware of the nature of the EU institutions and of their legal obligations – and the fundamental fact that the EU is a rules-based legal system with elected representatives to help create the laws applying to all its people.

I should explain that, during my professional life, I have had a greater opportunity than most to observe this at close quarters, having started working at the European Commission in February 1976, starting as a 'stagiaire' (trainee) before becoming a full-time administrator on both commercial and agricultural policy for a seven-year period. On leaving the European Commission in June 1984, I was elected as an MEP for the European Parliament constituency of Oxford and Buckinghamshire. I remained an elected MEP for 30 years before voluntarily standing down in June 2014.

The general lack of understanding of the EU was nicely put

in an article in *The Times* by Simon Nixon, who commented, 'The reason why the Brexit debate has gone round in circles for the past two years – and why the UK's negotiations have been almost completely stalled for months – is that much of the British political class have never fully understood what the EU is or how it works.'[1] He ended the piece by indicating that the UK had failed to cooperate effectively within the EU's systems:

> The British political class increasingly resembles a British tourist asking a foreigner for directions: unable to make itself understood, it simply shouts louder. Complaints about EU "theologians" only reveal a worrying lack of understanding of the realities of an organisation of which the UK was a member for 43 years. If Britain is to avoid finding itself unexpectedly stranded without a deal in March, it will need to start learning the language.[2]

On being elected as a MEP in June 1984, I found myself with a European Parliament constituency of around half a million voters stretching across the Thames Valley. The experience was a sharp learning curve, but I had the good fortune to share a parliamentary office in Amersham with the MP Ian Gilmour, Baron Gilmour of Craigmillar (who was then Sir Ian Gilmour), as well as benefitting from the advice of a canny political agent, Robert Nairne. Furthermore, not only did I have the luck to be a full-time member of the Budget Committee in Brussels, but I also started a regional network called TARGET to promote training in skills and technologies with my neighbouring MEP (my mother, Baroness Elles!). As it turned out, TARGET was a highly successful venture reaching more than 5,000 small and medium-sized enterprises across the Thames Valley, linking businesses with colleges and training providers.

But my incoming enthusiasm to do things for my voters in the Thames Valley was soon dampened by some advice which I received from the Party Chairman at the time, Norman Tebbit, during a visit to 10 Downing Street to meet the Prime Minister, Margaret Thatcher, with my MEP colleagues. When I told him about my interest in doing things for constituents, he said to me privately, 'Don't bother with that. That is not your task. Your duty is to tell those in Brussels what we think of them. We will look after the rest!'

There is more to be said about the nature and effectiveness of EU parliamentary democracy (see Chapter 2), but for now the question to answer is why it was that there could be several changes to the European treaties, changing the way in which our country is governed, with so little explanation to the British people about the EU institutions, and specifically the role of MEPs in UK public life – including awareness of the impacts of EU rules and regulations on Britons' lives, and the degree to which their ability to trade, travel and do business in Europe has been founded on them. Essentially, the fiction was maintained that Britain had joined an economic entity which had no political consequences.

UK entry into the EEC and the subsequent 1975 referendum

Initial statements by Prime Ministers of the two leading political parties at the time recognised that British member-ship of the European Economic Community (EEC) – which had been created by the Treaty of Rome in 1957 – would have political consequences. Labour Prime Minister Harold Wilson said:

> Whatever the economic arguments, the House will realise that, as I have repeatedly made clear, the Government's purpose derives above all from our recognition that Europe is now faced with the opportunity of a great move forward in political unity and that we can – and indeed must – play our full part in it.[3]

Later, Conservative Prime Minister Edward Heath wrote in *The Illustrated London News*:

> The community which we are joining is far more than a common market. It is a community in the true sense of that term. It is concerned not only with the establishment of free trade, economic and monetary union and other major economic issues – important though these are – but also ... with social issues which affect us all.[4]

In the House of Commons debates in the lead-up to UK membership of the EEC, Social Democratic Party founder David Owen agreed with Enoch Powell that the issue of cession of parliamentary sovereignty could not be disputed:

> Of course that means that one gives up sovereignty, and a lot of the debate in this House has been focussed upon sovereignty, and rightly so, because this is a central matter to many of the people who fundamentally do not wish us to

go into Europe. They do not wish to give up any measure of sovereignty .... It is, however, foolish to try to sell the concept of the EEC, and not admit that this means giving up some sovereignty.[5]

The real disagreement was over what pooling of sovereignty meant in practice. Heath argued that the conception of sovereignty was too narrow:

It is right that there should have been so much discussion of sovereignty .... If sovereignty exists to be used and to be of value, it must be effective. We have to make a judgment whether this is the most advantageous way of using our country's sovereignty.[6]

Writing on the debates in 2016, public policy consultant Greg Rosen summarised the nature of the controversy:

At the heart of this debate was not deception but genuine disagreement, over whether the economic benefits of EEC membership combined with the opportunity for greater collective power through pooled sovereignty outweighed the infringement upon narrow national sovereignty that EEC membership entailed.[7]

In the subsequent debates on the June 1975 referendum – which asked the public, 'Do you think the United Kingdom should stay in the European Community (the Common Market)?' – Prime Minister Harold Wilson won sufficient concessions from the EEC to enable a vote of two-thirds in favour of remaining. On this occasion, much of the Yes campaign focussed on the credentials of its opponents. According to Alistair McAlpine, the Yes campaign treasurer, 'The whole thrust of our campaign was to depict the anti-Marketeers as unreliable people – dangerous people who would lead you down the wrong path.'[8]

In Conservative campaign notes, a message from Margaret Thatcher, Party Leader at the time and campaigning to stay in, underlined that "the Community gives us a chance to influence world affairs. Britain's instincts have never been isolationist and membership of the Community enables us to play a full part in the counsels of Europe and a continuing role in the affairs of the world".[9]

So the referendum was won by a large majority, with a well-organised campaign in favour of staying in the EEC, but downplaying the question of sovereignty. Indeed, the Conservative Party's Yes campaign literature noted that Britain had already "pooled her nuclear capacity under the auspices of NATO and undertaken to share her oil supplies by the terms of the International Energy Programme". It also said that "every member state effectively has a veto on all matters of vital national interest raised in the Council of Ministers. The powers of the Commission are confined largely to administrative matters".[10] Thus, at the start of our EEC membership, it was certainly implied that we were joining more than a free trade arrangement. After all, as Jean Monnet had pointed out in 1962, you could not operate a common market without 'common rules applied by joint institutions'.[11] Furthermore, it was well known at the time that there were draft plans for the EEC to move ahead towards economic and monetary union (as per the Werner Report, which was presented in 1970).

However, if there was recognition of the general destination of the European project, a statement by the Prime Minister at the time of entry did little to clarify what the ultimate consequences for Britain might be. In a television broadcast, Heath said, 'There are some in this country who fear that going into Europe we shall in some way sacrifice independence and sovereignty. These fears, I need hardly say, are completely unjustified.'[12]

As time went on, there were those who highlighted vigorously the absence of clarity concerning sovereignty. In 2001, the journalist Christopher Booker cogently argued that efforts were made time and again to conceal what was really going on as the European project developed on the continent. The real long-term aim, he pointed out, was always that the countries of Western Europe should eventually come together in complete political and economic union:

> Britain's politicians have at every stage along the way, had to go through that process with which we are now so wearingly familiar: whereby first they express opposition to much of what their continental partners are proposing; then find themselves having to agree to more than they intended; and finally have to hide from the British people just how much they have given away .... The real problem for the British has been that, from the moment our politicians first decided in the 1960s and 1970s that we should join the project, they have never dared to admit openly to the British people that this was its true nature and purpose.[13]

There recently came to light a Foreign & Commonwealth

Office document that provides an insight into what a senior official expected to happen once Britain joined the EEC. In essence, the classified paper – dated April 1971 and locked away for decades under the Official Secrets Act – predicted the emergence of an economic and monetary union as well as a common foreign and security policy. The author also alluded to the fact that the increased role of Brussels would lead to a 'popular feeling of alienation from Government'.[14]

Stephen Wall summarised perfectly this conundrum. He concluded in his book *A Stranger in Europe* that while many of those involved in taking the UK into the EEC understood the political implications, those who came afterwards deliberately chose not to, often for narrow reasons of short-term political advantage.[15]

Critical treaty changes during UK membership of the EU

Given that the course was set among the British political class that the essence of sovereignty would not be lost through UK membership of the EEC, it is not surprising that tensions gradually mounted over the years as one revision to the Treaty of Rome succeeded another. Five changes were ratified by the House of Commons between 1987 and 2009, all transferring more competences to the EU institutions and, at the same time, giving incremental powers to the European Parliament to ensure more effective democratic legitimacy and accountability in the EU institutions (see Chapter 2).

The original idea behind the EEC was to achieve a union of European countries with common economic goals, avoiding once and for all further wars on the European continent.

By the mid 1980s, the members of the European club wanted to drive towards the goal of the single market through signing the Single European Act in 1986 (it was ratified in 1987). A European area without frontiers would be created, enabling the free movement of goods, services, people and capital. This was the first major change to the Treaty of Rome. The Prime Minister, Margaret Thatcher, was an enthusiast for breaking down barriers to trade that were of a regulatory nature. But the political consequences of the Single European Act do not seem to have been taken fully into account or explained – specifically the fact that, as a result of the shift to more majority-voting decision-making, Brussels and the European institutions would become more powerful.

The second treaty change of a fundamental nature was the Maastricht Treaty, signed in 1992 and effective from November 1993. It underpinned the basic shift from the EEC to the EU, introducing a number of substantive changes through a three-pillar structure. The first pillar was the European Communities, including an economic and monetary union, from which the UK could opt out. The second pillar was the Common Foreign and Security Policy. The third was Police and Judicial Cooperation in Criminal Matters (the development of cooperation in the fields of justice and home affairs), where, again, the UK had an opt-out. At this time, the concept of being a citizen of the EU was introduced.

The third treaty change was the Treaty of Amsterdam, signed in October 1997, that principally focussed on alterations that would be required for the enlargement of the EU to incorporate countries of Central and Eastern Europe. It entered into force in 1999, and made changes in the areas of fundamental rights, employment and the free movement of people. Hot on its heels was the fourth major change, the Treaty of Nice, signed in 2001, also preparing for eastward expansion and resulting in an EU of 25 rather than 15 member states. This involved structural change and streamlining decision-making processes.

The fifth and last major change was the Treaty of Lisbon, which followed the unsuccessful attempt to introduce the Treaty Establishing a Constitution for Europe that was rejected by French and Dutch voters in 2005. The Treaty of Lisbon, signed in 2007, amended the Maastricht Treaty (now officially called the Treaty on European Union) and also renamed the Treaty of Rome (which became the Treaty on the Functioning of the European Union). It eventually came into force in December 2009, having initially been rejected by Ireland in a 2008 referendum. The Irish resubmitted the treaty to their voters in a second referendum in 2009, having been given certain guarantees regarding EU action in sensitive areas of national competence, and the treaty was approved.

An aside on ratification: in the case of the Maastricht Treaty, which ushered in the single currency, Denmark, France and Ireland held referendums as required by their constitutions. On that occasion, Denmark narrowly failed to ratify the treaty in its referendum of 1992. Following the addition of the Edinburgh Agreement, which granted Denmark four exceptions to the Maastricht Treaty, a second Danish referendum in 1993 led to successful ratification. Ratification of the treaty was only narrowly won in France through its referendum in 1992. This result prompted Jacques Delors – President of the European Commission at the time – to comment that 'Europe began as an elitist project in which it was believed that all that was required was to convince the decision-makers. That phase of benign despotism is over'.[16]

In accordance with British constitutional convention, specifically that of parliamentary sovereignty, ratification by the UK was not subject to approval by referendum. Despite this fact, experts at the time considered that there was 'a clear constitutional rationale for requiring a referendum', based on the allocation of legislative power.[17] Regardless of the legal situation, what is striking is that no UK government sought the approval of the British people on constitutional changes which would substantially alter the way they would live their lives. This was definitely not restricted to one party alone. The Blair government's famous U-turn on holding a referendum on the proposed Treaty Establishing a Constitution for Europe is well documented; in his turn, Conservative Party Leader David Cameron gave a 'cast-iron' assurance in 2007 that he would allow a vote on the Treaty of Lisbon should he come into government:

> Today, I will give this cast-iron guarantee: if I become Prime Minister, a Conservative government will hold a ref- erendum on any EU treaty that emerges from these nego- tiations. No Treaty should be ratified without consulting the British people in a referendum.[18]

He reneged on this pledge shortly before the 2010 general election.

We took a very different path from the two countries which joined the EEC with us on 1st January 1973, Denmark and

Ireland. Like the UK, these two countries have proud histories and are strongly independent in nature. I was to learn directly about their feelings when I went to Copenhagen in 2013 to speak at a rally to celebrate the 40th anniversary of all three countries joining the EEC. While I represented the British point of view, the former Taoiseach John Bruton represented the Irish, and the Danish perspective was given by the former Foreign Minister Niels Helveg Petersen. When the question arose of why there was a strong Eurosceptic movement in the UK with regard to the EU while the situation in Denmark and Ireland was more quiescent, the clear answer was that regular consultation of the Danish and Irish people had headed off real grievances because they had been given the opportunity to have their say (not always without controversy).

The French President François Mitterrand took a subtler approach to explain the concept of the European dimension to the French people. In a televised speech on 30th March 1987, to celebrate the 30th anniversary of the signing of the Treaty of Rome, he had both the French tricolour and the European flag standing beside him as he spoke. While the tricolour represented the traditions of the French people, he said, the European flag represented their future. Thenceforth, every presidential speech would be made with the two flags present.

Although the treaty changes had been agreed democratically, with an approving vote on each occasion by the House of Commons, the British people were none the wiser about the increasing influence of EU law on their lives. Very little effort was made to explain EU institutions in classrooms, or to bring MEPs into the daily life of the nation (see Chapter 2). This was doubly regrettable as the UK always had less of a natural feeling for European unity than other EU member states, not only because of its imperial history and the resultant Commonwealth, but also due to not having suffered a major invasion for nearly a thousand years. The instincts of continental countries were more open to an ever-closer union, not least to ensure that Germany was a full part of their shared sovereignty.

Instead, as time passed, it became more and more common for UK politicians to blame Brussels for everything that went wrong, with strong support from many of the tabloids owned by foreign nationals. It is still almost impossible to access the major TV channels of other member states in the UK, as these are not available on Sky. Sadly, this meant that although other member states made the effort to explain that joint European efforts were worthwhile, as concerns on major issues were shared across frontiers, these messages were rarely received in Britain... lost in translation!

Looking back today, it is a matter of real regret that none of these treaty changes was ever put to a vote of the British people by the government of the day. I firmly believe they should have been. What might have been possible in the 20th century with restricted access to news is no longer possible with the reach of the internet today, which definitely encourages a broader, more inclusive approach. Small wonder that many people in Britain did not understand which powers were attributed to EU institutions, and the ways in which they were accountable. This was to be a decisive factor in the result of the 2016 EU membership referendum in which the stated aim of the Leave campaign was to 'Take Back Control'.

The second referendum, 2016

It is ironic to note that the first referendum, called by the Labour Party in 1975, was intended to avoid a major split in the party over Europe. The second referendum, called in 2016 by the Conservative Party, was essentially called for similar internal reasons. Cameron, the Conservative Party Leader, certainly hoped that it would do the trick. But he was too ambitious, and massively failed. Perhaps he should have had a simple in/out referendum in the autumn of 2015 without any promises of treaty revision. In the flush of a general election victory, there are many who think he would have been successful had he opted for this direct approach, avoiding being drawn into an ultimately unsuccessful renegotiation of the treaties.

The run-up to the campaign

A treaty change that had a significant impact on the British people was one which dealt with migration. Early in 2004, with the enlargement of the EU to incorporate ten countries from Central and Eastern Europe, most member states took the sensible precaution to limit, under permitted transitional provisions, any possible large-scale movement of people from the new member states. Sadly, this was not the case in the UK, where the Blair government decided to allow a free flow on the assumption that about 13,000 people would come in the first year of entry. Within 18 months, more than 500,000 came. Too many new arrivals, too fast, simply created huge tensions in British society, generating for millions of British citizens a sense of loss of identity, and anxiety about the pace and scale of ethnic change. This, along with the Great Recession, was the perfect theme for the ascendant UK Independence Party (UKIP) to exploit – as was illustrated by the vast increase in its level of representation in the European Parliament, rising from 12 seats in 2004 to 24 in 2014.

The calling of a second referendum was not a certainty, but it became unavoidable as pressure built up on the Conservative Party to deal with the rise of UKIP. The story of how the party came to be the standard bearer for the referendum is told by the MEP Daniel Hannan in his recent book *What Next?: How to get the best from Brexit*. Starting from a small base, the People's Pledge campaign, which had cross-party support, capitalised on the economic recession – and people's disquiet of EU decisions taken to hold the euro together – to apply pressure and bring about a referendum on EU membership. Voters were asked to pledge that they would use their votes in the next general election to 'secure a majority of MPs in Parliament who support an EU referendum'. As a result, in January 2013 Cameron promised a referendum in a speech at Bloomberg.[19] This pledge to hold an in/out referendum on EU membership was then included in the Conservative manifesto for the May 2015 general election. After the Conservative Party emerged victorious as the largest party in the House of Commons, Cameron formed the new Conservative government and decided to move quickly to implement the promised referendum. The fact that he was no longer in coalition with the Liberal Democrats meant that he had no reason to delay its implementation. In the autumn of 2015, proposals for the holding of a referendum were submitted to the House of Commons and passed by a huge majority – this was a decision for which all were responsible.

In carrying out the election pledge and drawing up the provisions for the vote, however, Cameron showed little attention to detail. It was decided that those aged 16–17 years would not have a vote, although they had been included in the referendum for Scottish independence a year earlier. British citizens who had been resident abroad for a certain number of years were also ineligible to vote, even though they would be the people most likely to be affected by the outcome. Furthermore, no provisions were put in place to have a minimum threshold in recognition that this was an important constitutional vote. And, extraordinarily, although the referendum was an advisory vote, the government (presumably ultra-confident that the Leave campaign could never succeed) indicated its willingness to accept the result. The government certainly did not make any preparations for a Leave win.

As the domestic rules for the referendum were put in place, Cameron zigzagged his way across Europe, trying to find supporters for introducing the reforms he recommended in his Bloomberg speech. No one among his close advisers seems to have told him that this was never going to be the moment for calling an Intergovernmental Conference to open up the EU's founding treaties to be amended, as many countries were still suffering the economic consequences of the Great Recession. There would, in any case, be no way of getting the changes he had requested through their democratic procedures. Without treaty changes, his Bloomberg speech recommendations were dead in the water. Furthermore, when Cameron arrived in Brussels for the final discussions on a possible deal, the EU was facing a huge international migrant crisis. There was a real prospect of millions of refugees pouring into Southern

Europe from Turkey, Iraq, Syria or Libya. A pause for thought would have told any sensible person that campaigning for a referendum in these emotive circumstances was a hugely risky undertaking.

Not surprisingly, the negotiations ended in failure, because British negotiators – not for the first time – overestimated their abilities to influence the other EU member states, particularly Germany. There was always the feeling that the British view would best prevail through direct discussions with leaders from other member states. There was too little experience or knowledge among British politicians and their political advisers of European politics and personalities and EU legislative processes. Officials would be better informed than those they advised, but lacked their political authority and failed to win their trust. This would become very visible later on during the negotiations for the departure of the UK from the EU.

The referendum campaign

The campaign for Remain started well enough, focussing on the economic benefits of staying in the EU. As time passed, however, the campaign became so entangled in extreme economic projections about what would happen should Britain leave (a tactic that was disparaged by Brexiteers as 'Project Fear') that it lost credibility. By contrast, a poster launched by the Leave campaign in early June threatening a major migrant invasion had a huge impact in certain parts of Britain, the fear of migration encouraging many to vote to leave. As the campaigns progressed, Remain's lack of vision became evident, even if it was well known that younger voters were predominantly in favour of staying in. The Remain campaign failed to highlight the need for European countries to work together to take a common stand against rising Chinese influence, a growing challenge to Western societies (see Chapter 3). Last but not least, the Remain campaign surprisingly made no effort to explain the nature of shared sovereignty or the political dimension of the EU, and never clearly rebutted the Leave campaign's oft-quoted claim that the EU institutions were unelected and unaccountable.

Robin Niblett, Director of Chatham House, made a significant contribution on the issue of sovereignty before the campaign got underway. He noted that many in Britain believed that the EU decision-making process had undermined British parliamentary democracy, and that leaving the EU was the only way for the British people to regain control of their sovereignty. This, he argued, ignored the fact that successive British governments had chosen to pool aspects of the country's sovereign power in the EU in order to achieve national objectives that they could not have achieved on their own:

Is it time ... to return economic and political sovereign power entirely to Westminster? The risks of doing so are extensive. For example, the UK would be excluded from the process of EU rule-writing, making it a less attractive location for foreign investment. The UK is unlikely to strike better trade deals alone than it has currently through the EU. And the UK would have no say in the design of more open EU markets for digital, financial and other services .... In a world that is more interdependent today than it was when the UK joined the European Economic

Community in 1973, the notion of "absolute" British sovereignty is illusory .... Judging from the UK's experience
and its future prospects, the opportunities from remaining
in the EU far outweigh the risks of doing so, and the risks
of leaving far outweigh the opportunities.[20]

A revealing article on the question of sovereignty was contrib-
uted by Vernon Bogdanor, writing about why the EU keeps
destroying Conservative Prime Ministers. He drew attention
to the fact that Britain's profound differences from the Continent and long evolutionary history are reflected in the notion
of the sovereignty of Parliament, a concept alien to continental Europe, which must be distinguished from the concept
of national sovereignty with which it is often confused.
Bogdanor wrote, 'It is the notion of Parliamentary sovereignty
which makes it so difficult for Britain to subordinate herself to
a superior legal order such as that of the EU.'[21]

Leading the Remain campaign, however, Cameron never
once took the opportunity to explain the concept of shared
sovereignty whereby our elected representatives, MEPs, have
been directly involved in making legislative and budgetary
decisions to ensure the accountability of the EU institutions.
Indeed, a bet put forward by an MEP colleague of mine prom-
ising to give £50 to anyone who heard Cameron mention the
European Parliament was never met. After the campaign,
Cameron had the honesty to declare that he never really liked
the European Parliament. One could legitimately ask: why
was he heading a pro-European campaign in the first place?

In a notable difference from the equivalent campaign in
the 1975 referendum, very little effort was made to demonise

those who were running the Leave campaign. It appeared that Cameron took pains not to fall out with his close colleagues Gove and Johnson; presumably he thought this would not be conducive to governing after the referendum, and that it was unnecessary, as Remain was going to win anyway. Gove and Johnson's decisions to take active roles in the Leave campaign gave it a respectability which it would not have achieved solely with Farage.

In retrospect, if the Remain campaign held most of the cards, it did not have the laser-like focus of the Leave campaign, or its determination to win. In place of the vague 'Go Global' motto originally proposed, Leave zeroed in on its theme, 'Take Back Control' – thus the claim that the £350 million payment made per week to the EU could be given instead to the NHS. But no effort was made to agree the details of the UK–EU relationship once Britain was outside the EU. Dominic Cummings, the Campaign Director for Leave, remarked:

> What would have been the point of that?! Approximately nobody knows anything about the important details of how the EU works including the MPs who have spent years talking about it and the journalists who cover it .... I am not aware of a single MP or political journalist who understands the Single Market.[22]

Instead, Leave focussed its campaigning on three big forces having global impact: the immigration crisis, the financial crisis and the euro crisis. It minimised poster campaigning, devoting almost all of its funds to digital channels – now well known due to its militarisation of data with the help of Cambridge Analytica and AggregateIQ. Leave knew only too well that funds spent on digital would be less easily monitored than offline expenditure.

The aftermath

If the outcome of the vote was reasonably close, with 51.8% to Leave compared to 48.2% for Remain, the turnout (at around 72%) was massive compared to normal general elections. Even so, a petition calling for a rerun, signed by over 4 million people, was handed in shortly after the referendum, as many felt that Leave had won on false pretences. The unexpected result led to political upheaval, with the resignation of Cameron and the success of Theresa May in becoming Conservative Party Leader and Prime Minister in his place. From the outset, there was the possibility, given the narrowness of the result, to seek a broad all-party approach, as this was a national decision which split both parties. But the incoming Prime Minister vowed in her speech to the Conservative Party conference in October 2016 to take a tough line in the negotiations, setting out clear red lines: the UK would be outside the single market and the customs union, with no interference from the European Court of Justice, and it would cease large payments to the EU. (It is rumoured that this speech was drafted by Nick Timothy, the chief of staff to the Prime Minister, with little consultation of senior civil servants or members of the Cabinet.) These lines were confirmed in follow-up speeches at Lancaster House, in Florence and at Mansion House. This hard-line approach was to affect the course of the negotiations as it gave the British negotiators very little room for manoeuvre. Many consider that the final withdrawal agreement reached was the best that could be achieved for British interests in the circumstances.

Although it was a logical step to give the major positions for conducting the negotiations to those prominent in the Leave campaign (Gove, Johnson, David Davis and Liam Fox), it did not necessarily provide the UK team with all the expertise needed to produce a successful outcome. Indeed, it has become clear that this has been a massive learning process for leading Conservative politicians. Among the principal Leavers, perhaps buoyed by the elation of the moment, hyperbole followed hyperbole, with claims being made that we would have more Europe rather than less (Johnson); that the UK–EU talks would be completed within the year (Davis); and that major trade deals would be easy to negotiate (Fox).

In the autumn of 2016, against virulent opposition, the UK Houses of Parliament won the right to have their say before triggering Article 50 to leave the EU over a two-year period. Nevertheless, it was triggered in March 2017. The Brexit Secretary at that time, David Davis, said that there would be a major battle about the order in which issues would be negotiated, with parallel trade talks alongside the main withdrawal agreement. This was no more than a damp squib. Article 50 (below) sets out that the withdrawal treaty was the main item to be discussed, with only the need to take into account the framework for the future relationship.

Article 50 – Treaty on European Union
1. Any Member State may decide to withdraw from the Union in accordance with its own constitutional requirements.

2. A Member State which decides to withdraw shall notify the European Council of its intention. In the light of the guidelines provided by the European Council, the Union shall negotiate and conclude an agreement with that State, setting out the arrangements for its withdrawal, taking account of the framework for its future relationship with the Union. That agreement shall be negotiated in accordance with Article 218(3) of the Treaty on the Functioning of the European Union. It shall be concluded on behalf of the Union by the Council, acting by a qualified majority, after obtaining the consent of the European Parliament.

3. The Treaties shall cease to apply to the State in question from the date of entry into force of the withdrawal agreement or, failing that, two years after the notification referred to in paragraph 2, unless the European Council, in agreement with the Member State concerned, unanimously decides to extend this period.

4. For the purposes of paragraphs 2 and 3, the member of the European Council or of the Council representing the withdrawing Member State shall not participate in the discussions of the European Council or Council or in decisions concerning it.

   A qualified majority shall be defined in accordance with Article 238(3)(b) of the Treaty on the Functioning of the European Union.

5. If a State which has withdrawn from the Union asks to rejoin, its request shall be subject to the procedure referred to in Article 49.[23]

The former diplomat Lord Kerr, who was a member of the European Convention that first drafted what became Article 50, said in 2017 that the article 'is about paying the bills, settling one's commitments, dealing with acquired rights, thinking about the pensions. It's not an article about the future relationship'.[24] This did not stop senior government figures believing that they would have a full trade agreement buttoned down by March 2019. Lord Kerr also commented that he had never thought that Article 50 would be triggered by the UK, expecting it to be utilised by a member state taken over by an authoritarian leader.[25]

As the negotiations took shape in the spring of 2017, the Prime Minister took the fateful decision to call a General Election in June 2017, with the Conservative Party well ahead in the polls. The result of this election was to deprive the government of its majority and force it to rely on the support of the Democratic Unionist Party (DUP). This was a turning point, making the realisation of Brexit even more difficult to secure. By the end of December 2017, a withdrawal agreement was agreed in outline, and it included the proposal of the backstop for Ireland. This allowed the decision to be taken to start discussions on the outline future trade agreement, recognising that the withdrawal agreement needed to be incorporated into law (whereas the trade document would be non-binding).

In retrospect, it is astonishing that the issue of Ireland did not figure more prominently during the campaign. When asked about the question of a new border, Daniel Hannan gave a typical Brexiteer reply, saying, 'Would the border between the UK and Northern Ireland return? Would the peace process be jeopardised? There is, of course, zero prospect of either happening, and I said so. London and Dublin have never enjoyed warmer relations than now.'[26] It did not seem to strike him that leaving a zone covered by EU law would cause a major problem for the authorities on both sides of the border.

During the first six months of 2018, Davis, as Britain's chief Brexit negotiator, apparently only had four hours of talks with his opposite number, Michel Barnier. Instead, he devoted more time to touring European capitals to sound out member state leaders as European Council members. After technical discussions on what an agreement might include, the idea of the Chequers Agreement was born in July 2018, under the authority of the Prime Minister, May.[27]

Its supporters claimed that the Chequers Agreement was the only satisfactory way to implement the result of the referendum, maintaining the concept of frictionless trade with a complicated Facilitated Customs Arrangement for collecting duties, and a common area for goods – but not services – through a common rulebook. This remained an anathema to many who felt that it kept the UK too closely bound to the EU. It was also rejected by the EU for being too much like cherry-picking and tearing up the functioning of the single market, separating goods from services and allowing for frictionless trade without common supervision by the European Commission and ultimate enforcement by the European Court of Justice. However, a revised form of this approach concluded the negotiations with what is now known as the withdrawal agreement, running to nearly 600 pages. It was agreed by the European Council at a special meeting on 25th November 2018.[28] The final form of a future UK–EU trade relationship was kept open in the accompanying political declaration, which runs to around 30 pages. But signing up to the withdrawal agreement makes the UK what is defined by the EU as a 'third country' – it ensures that Brexit is achieved, but means that the UK still takes on most EU laws without having a say on them (see Chapter 3).[29]

It was never going to be simple to get the withdrawal agreement through the House of Commons with a government only capable of surviving thanks to the votes of the DUP. A meaningful vote on the withdrawal agreement, originally intended to be taken before Christmas 2018, was postponed until the second half of January 2019. It was then defeated by a margin of 230 votes, with many MPs worried that the provisions of the backstop would keep the UK permanently in a customs union with the EU. A second meaningful vote, held in March 2019, was also defeated, this time by a margin of 149 votes. Extraordinary procedures then took place to determine whether Parliament could agree through indicative votes on a different way forward, but these votes failed to find a solution. Finally, a third meaningful vote was taken just before the end of March, and it too failed to get through. Even a late outreach to the Labour Party to get its backing for the deal was unable to succeed, as Conservative MPs baulked at the idea of a permanent customs union as well as a confirmatory referendum on the deal. So with the extension of the Leave date to 31st October and the new Conservative leader, Boris Johnson, in charge, it will be up to him and the new government to pick up the negotiations – soon with a newly installed EU team – and find a way through the maze.

After the first meaningful vote fell, the President of the

European Council, Donald Tusk, remarked that there would be a special place reserved in hell for those who had campaigned to withdraw without having a clear idea of what they wanted.[30] I suspect there will be many others who wish for the same fate to meet those who thought that a referendum on EU membership at this juncture and under the conditions set was the best way to resolve the problems of the UK's membership of the EU.

When reviewing the story of Britain's membership of the EU, the conclusion must be reached that there was a real reluctance among the British political class to reveal the reach of EU institutions in the daily lives of those living in Britain. Avoiding further referendums at the time of each of the five EU treaty changes meant that the concept of parliamentary sovereignty could be maintained, but left the British people in the dark as to who was responsible for what.

This notion of lack of awareness of EU policies was at the heart of the Leave campaign, as has now become clear after the referendum. This also encompasses understanding the nature of Article 50, which is about settling one's commitments, not about the future relationship.

The hard-line approach taken by the British government, with its four red lines set in October 2016, shaped the outcome of the withdrawal agreement, with a view to maintaining frictionless trade for goods while keeping the Irish border open. Had this agreement been passed at the third time of asking, the UK would now be out of the EU, but it failed principally because it did not get the backing of some of those who had demanded the red lines in the first place. They continue to aspire to a Canada-style free-trade relationship giving them the freedom to negotiate global trade deals, hoping that the EU will maintain frictionless trade between the UK and the single market while finding a technological solution to the Irish border (see Chaper 3).

2

Fact

The unwillingness of British leaders to explain the nature of EU institutions and the political implications of EU membership is well established. It is impossible to recall any major speech by a British Prime Minister from 1973 onwards explaining the EU institutions and the implications of shared sovereignty for the origin of many of the laws we apply today in our country. Indeed, one of the most remarkable comments during the 2016 referendum campaign period was the claim by Gove that the European Parliament was a mock parliament.[31]

To understand EU democracy, it is necessary to comprehend the nature of the EU institutions, not least the role of the EU leaders in the European Council setting the strategic direction of the institutions; the growing influence and powers of the European Parliament in the EU process; and the differing ways in which MEPs link to their national legislatures (particularly in the UK).

The nature of the EU institutions
Much of the problem for Britons seeking to understand the EU institutions lies in their different structure of governance compared to that in most member states (which is typically that of government versus opposition). In the EU, the

structure is much more similar to that of the US, with a separation of the executive and the legislature.

As is well known in the US, the President is directly elected, and members of the bicameral system of the Senate and the House are chosen through regular elections every two years. While all members of the House are elected on a two-year basis, senators serve a six-year term. As is also known, members of the US Cabinet are appointed by the US President, with hearings in the Senate for confirmation of appointment. Members of the US Cabinet are expressly forbidden by the US constitution to stand for election in Congress. What will be less well known is that the EU system is similar. The EU treaties also insist on a separation of powers between the executive and the legislature. Thus commissioners – members of the European Commission – are forbidden to stand for election for the European Parliament, but like their US counterparts they have to go through open hearings in the European Parliament before being given confirmation to take office. Although not directly elected, the European Commission President has to be voted in by an absolute majority of newly elected MEPs before formally entering office after being chosen by EU leaders in the European Council, by a qualified majority vote.

As highlighted in Table 1, the European Council is composed of the elected heads of government of the member states, overseen by an appointed President. The treaties dictate that the European Council has no legislative function, but provides impetus for the development of the EU and defines its political directions and priorities. Governments are also in the Council of the European Union, sharing powers with the

European Parliament in making decisions on new laws proposed by the European Commission. A simple explanation of the building blocks of the EU's construction is clearly set out in a book by John McCormick called *Why Europe Matters: The Case for the European Union*. He explains that the EEC was established in the 1950s with common institutions to achieve the economic goals assigned. At the time, there was an appointed Commission, an appointed European Court of Justice and a weak and unelected European Parliament. The focus of decision-making lay with the Council of Ministers, where national interests continued to be defended by government ministers. Today, the EU institutions are structured as indicated in Table 1.

It is important to grasp how the nature of the institutions of the EU has changed within a 40-year period in order to understand why these institutions have had such an effect on the lives of the British people. They are not like a sports club to which a subscription is paid with the option of terminating it at a whim. They are rules-based, law-making bodies. These institutions are a judicious mix of an intergovernmental and supranational nature, as is further demonstrated by the following passage from McCormick's book:

> The European Union is an organisation whose work is in the hands of institutions whose members are either elected by European voters, appointed by national governments, or are drawn directly from those national governments. So while we can say that the EU is more than a conventional international organisation, and while there has been much pooling or sharing of policy responsibilities, the

Table 1: A guide to the EU institutions [32]

Institution	Membership	Character	Function
European Council	Elected heads of government of the member states, overseen by an appointed President	Intergovernmental	A steering committee charged with making broad decisions on the process of integration
European Commission	Commissioners nominated by national governments, overseeing 40,000 career bureaucrats	Supranational	Proposes new laws and policies, and oversees their execution once enacted by the Council of the EU and Parliament
Council of the European Union	Government ministers from the member states	Intergovernmental	Shares power with Parliament over the enactment of proposals for new laws
European Parliament	Elected representatives from the member states	Supranational	Shares power with the Council of the EU over the enactment of proposals for new laws
European Court of Justice	Judges appointed by the member states	Supranational	Ensures that the actions of individuals, organisations and governments fit with the terms of the treaties

EU falls some way short of being a federal United States of Europe, and – most importantly – there is direct or indirect accountability to European voters all along the way. That Brussels has accumulated independent powers and has the ability to make decisions without the input of national governments or their representatives is one of the enduring fictions about Europe. Thus when Nigel Farage, leader of UKIP, charged in 2012 that the outcome of the next election in Britain was moot because 'we are not governed from Westminster, we are governed from Brussels', it was an overstatement bordering on the delirious.[33]

The development of the European Parliament

When the UK first joined the EEC, the European Parliament (or Assembly) was appointed by the governments of the member states. It was only in June 1979 that the first direct elections to the European Parliament took place. MEPs are elected under national electoral systems, but these have to observe certain common principles established in EU law, notably proportional representation. In some member states, voters can only vote for a list of candidates, with no possibility of changing the order of those candidates (closed list); in others, voters can express their preference for one or more of the candidates (preferential voting). Instead of a list system, some member states achieve the latter possibility of preferential voting by using the single transferable vote. Britain opted for the first of these options, a closed list system.

At its first election, the powers of the European Parliament were limited. Essentially, it had the right to give opinions on draft legislation and the power to reject the annual budget, but little else. Even so, the Conservative campaign guide noted the importance of the election:

> Perhaps the most important, although often forgotten, result of the gradual movement towards European unity since 1945 has been to make war between the western European states almost unthinkable .... the United Kingdom and the other member states of the Community are ... pooling their national sovereignty in certain agreed areas in order to secure a wider and more effective common sovereignty.[34]

In looking at how the European Parliament has evolved since the days of the first European election, it is instructive to examine its structure, its powers and its influence.

Structure

Today, the EU has 28 member states (or 27 upon the departure of the UK) with 23 languages, having expanded from its original six countries and four languages in 1957. (It should be noted that figures beyond May 2019 were not available at the time of publication, and are not used here.) The European Parliament has 751 MEPs, represented within eight political groups. These political groups, remaining broadly stable over the eight terms of the European Parliament to date, have provided the framework for national parties to function at a European level. But the number of these national parties has mushroomed from 168 in the 2004–2009 term to 232 in the 2014–2019 term, because of the extraordinary variety of representation in EU member states.

From 1979, the three biggest groups have been the European People's Party (EPP), the Progressive Alliance of Socialists and Democrats (S&D) and the European Conservatives and Reformists (ECR), having a majority of MEPs in the House until the last election. This has now altered, as the two largest groups – the EPP and the S&D – lost ground to the Liberals and the Greens in the European Parliament election of May 2019.

The main governing bodies of the European Parliament are the Bureau, the Conference of Presidents and the Conference of Committee Chairs. The Bureau is the body responsible for financial, organisational and administrative matters within the European Parliament, being composed of the President and the 14 Vice-Presidents, elected by an absolute majority of votes in plenary, with the order in which they attained that majority determining their order of preference. The Quaestors, also elected, look after the financial and administrative interests of Members of the European Parliament. The Conference of Presidents – composed of the European Parliament's President and the chairs of its eight political groups – sets the agenda of the plenary and determines the general political orientations of the institution. There are 20 standing committees (and two sub-committees), each covering a different policy area. They draw up reports for the plenary to consider (on both legislative and non-legislative matters) and hold the executive to account. Lastly, the Conference of Committee Chairs coordinates the work of the committees and ensures the smooth functioning between them.

Finally, it is notable that there is a substantive rate of member turnover at each European Parliament election.

Overall, of the 751 MEPs elected in 2014, 48.5% were new to the European Parliament. The average age of MEPs at the constituent session in July 2014 was 53 years, the oldest member hailing from Greece (aged 91) and the youngest from Denmark (aged 26). The evolution of the proportion of women among all MEPs at the beginning of each parliamentary term shows a gradual increase, rising from 16.3% in the first term and reaching 36.5% in the 2014–2019 term. This compares favourably with EU national parliaments, where the comparable figure across national parliaments was given in 2018 as 27.9%.[35]

Powers

Next, let us briefly look at the way in which the powers of the European Parliament have grown since the first direct elections in 1979. Starting from a base of a consultative nature, the European Parliament has become a co-legislator with the Council of the European Union. With every treaty revision, the powers of the European Parliament have been extended. The Treaty of Lisbon, which came into force in 2009, states, 'The European Parliament shall, jointly with the Council, exercise legislative and budgetary functions. It shall exercise functions of political control and consultation as laid down in the Treaties. It shall elect the President of the Commission.'[36] Thus, in the time that Britain has been an EU member, the European Parliament has changed from being consultative in nature to being a real legislative power. The legislative procedure covers such areas as economic governance, energy, transport, immigration, the environment and consumer affairs. Most European laws are adopted jointly by the European Parliament and the Council.

In addition to legislative competence, the European Parliament has over time become the equal partner of the Council on agreeing all aspects of the budget. This means that, within a long-term financial framework established by the budgetary authority over a seven-year period, the European Parliament and the Council share responsibility for the adoption of the annual budget. The European Commission then implements the budget. Furthermore, the European Parliament has the power to reject trade agreements and the right to be updated on the progress of negotiations by the Commission. The European Parliament also now has significant supervisory powers over the European Commission, with the power not only to reject individual Commissioners, but also to dismiss the Commission itself.

Influence

Finally, let us consider the increasing influence of the European Parliament in the lives of the 500-million-odd citizens of the EU in the budgetary, legislative and political fields. The first example is in the field of budgetary control, and concerns the case of the fall of the European Commission in March 1999. It is one with which I am personally very familiar, as it was my discharge report which triggered the Commission's historic resignation en masse. In brief, I was the overall rapporteur overseeing the 1996 budget through the European Parliament. At that time, it was customary that the same person should follow the budget through the subsequent discharge. During this latter process, it came to light that the Commission had problems with the functioning of programmes under its implementation, and had not taken sufficient action to ensure the necessary levels of staff required. Although the budget discharge was narrowly approved by the Committee on Budgetary Control, it was thrown out in the December 1998 plenary, triggering a process of reporting by the so-called 'Wise Men', the individuals appointed as independent witnesses to review the situation. Although the report found nothing novel about the situation confronting the Commission, it concluded with a phrase that was damning to the Commission and its leadership: 'It is becoming difficult to find anyone who has even the slightest sense of responsibility.'[37] The entire Commission decided to resign on 15th March 1999. The shake-up which then ensued concerning budgetary management in the Commission would never have happened without European Parliament power. The changes introduced tighter controls on expenditure as well as stricter limits on people recruited to work for Commissioners. The other half of the budgetary authority, the Council, had already given a green light to the Commission in the autumn of 1998!

The second example is a set of data showing how the European Parliament has used its legislative powers to ensure that the people's voices are heard: during the seventh parliamentary term, running from 2009–2014, nearly 44,000 amendments were proposed, of which over 21,000 were adopted. Nearly 3,000 texts were adopted along with over 1,000 legislative acts. Furthermore, MEPs as individual members tabled nearly 60,000 written questions.[38] In the eighth term so far, from July 2014 to December 2018, over 20,000 amendments were proposed. Of these, nearly 13,000 were adopted. MEPs tabled nearly 50,000 written questions.

Three procedures are used in amending and passing

legislation, the most common now being the 'ordinary legislative procedure', traditionally referred to as 'co-decision'. The Parliament may also be required to give (or withhold) its consent to certain Council decisions, or may simply be consulted on certain Commission proposals. Under co-decision and consent, the European Parliament has a right of veto over EU legal acts. Table 2 shows the rise in the use of co-decision, reflecting greater European Parliament power from successive treaty changes, and the growing trend for the European Parliament and Council to agree on legislative texts at the first reading of that process.

The European Parliament adopts its positions by voting in plenary sessions on legislative and budgetary texts, as well as on other resolutions. The standing committees undertake detailed consideration of draft legislation and hold public hearings on key issues. During the course of the legislative process, representatives of European Parliament committees meet frequently with their counterparts in the Council of the European Union and the European Commission, in negotiations known as trilogues, undertaken by policy issue.

One recent example of a piece of legislation debated and agreed by the European Parliament during the 2014–2019 mandate was the General Data Protection Regulation (GDPR), which entered into force in May 2018 after over 3,000 amendments were tabled to the draft proposal of the European Commission in the relevant European Parliament committees. Although it met considerable resistance among several interest groups, the GDPR has become a global pioneer for rules on privacy, with the US now considering whether to shape its own rules taking into account those now in force in the EU. Even those opposed to the final outcome cannot deny that the European Parliament acted as a wonderful generator of public debate on a highly sensitive and important issue.

Finally, a foreign policy issue of considerable concern was the so-called Anti-Counterfeiting Trade Agreement (ACTA) case, where the European Parliament vetoed the ACTA, using its power to reject trade agreements for the first time. When the Commission requested the European Parliament view, although the Council had already approved, the deal was rejected because of its effects on human rights.

As part of the powers that the European Parliament gained under the 2009 Treaty of Lisbon, it has the power to consent to the withdrawal of the UK from the EU. Thus the Commission's negotiator, Michel Barnier, has kept in touch on an almost daily basis with the European Parliament's Brexit negotiators to ensure their views are taken into account.

More examples of the impact of the European Parliament during the period 2014–2019 are provided in an in-depth analysis published by the European Parliamentary Research Service in April 2019.[40]

Many will wonder what an MEP does with their time. Following on from the duties outlined above, there are clear responsibilities for MEPs to influence decisions taken through budgetary or legislative acts that are applicable to all the people living in the EU, whether on environmental, consumer or social laws. There is also a representational duty similar to that carried out by MPs. Where an MP takes up matters relating to national law in Westminster on behalf of constituents, MEPs do the same for constituents on matters relating to European law, taking them up with the EU institutions by

Table 2: European Parliament legislative activity, 2004–2018 [39]

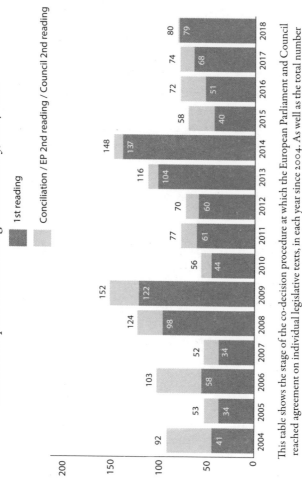

This table shows the stage of the co-decision procedure at which the European Parliament and Council reached agreement on individual legislative texts, in each year since 2004. As well as the total number of files agreed, the graph also shows the number agreed at first reading (the most common case).

using parliamentary questions, urgency resolutions and so on. In many instances I assisted constituents living in the Thames Valley, whether it was addressing problems arising with the Joint European Torus project (JET) at Culham and the European School nearby; promoting European schemes to facilitate training in new technologies across the Thames Valley; or, in one instance, helping a constituent transport her Palomino horse from Portugal to the UK. I also took the time to go to schools at their request to talk about the European dimension, and on occasion to help them plan visits to the EU institutions.

Linkages between the European Parliament and national parliaments: the UK case

The basic provisions of the treaties concerning such linkages are summarised in the Protocol on the Role of the National Parliaments in the European Union, agreed in 2010 as an addition to the Treaty of Lisbon. This document summarises the information to be made available to national parliaments on a regular basis, as well as providing a framework for international cooperation in the form of the Conference of Parliamentary Committees for Union Affairs of Parliaments of the European Union (COSAC).

Each member state has its own structure for scrutiny of EU legislation as well as its own rules about who is involved in such a process. The Belgian case is the most advanced in that it allows for EU legislation to be scrutinised by an equal number of MEPs alongside national parliamentarians, whereas there has been no involvement of MEPs in the UK case. National parliaments in other member states such as Ireland, Germany and Holland have regular close links with their MEPs. Indeed, this question of linkage preoccupied the attention of leading British politicians in the 1980s wondering how best to ensure that there was close contact between the legislatures. Some, like Lord Carrington, were sceptical and considered the European Parliament to be a talking shop. He found 'anomalous the idea of a European Parliament, with directly elected members, struggling to behave as if it were a sovereign parliament in a sovereign state. For the European Parliament ... cannot have power'. If it did have power, he said, 'this would bring it up against the authority of national governments, supported by national parliaments. They do have power'.[41]

A more pragmatic line was illustrated in a pamphlet written by Michael Heseltine called *The Democratic Deficit*, which was published in 1989. Not only did he examine 'a Europe of Parliaments' but also the European Parliament itself. He was unequivocal about the destiny of Europe, citing Sir Geoffrey Howe's 1972 statement in the House of Commons that 'the purpose of the application to join the Community is a fundamental and deliberate use of sovereignty to engage in sharing sovereignty to the greater advantage of all'. Heseltine added, 'He was right to say it then. The truth, far from withering with age, is starker today. The British Parliament voluntarily accepted a sharing of legal sovereignty when it passed the European Communities Act in 1972. The provisions of the Act allow no other interpretation.'[42] He was forthright about the consequences of this decision, writing, 'The frustration of national parliaments is very evident as they feel power slipping away, first to the Brussels bureaucracy and then, more recently, to the European Parliament. There is good cause for this anxiety, and we must address it.'[43]

His conclusion was that the House of Commons would have 'every interest in cooperating more closely with British MEPs'; the latter, he argued, had 'power to influence the shape of European legislation before it [became] fixed and legally binding on member states'.[44] The members of the national parliament had none. Heseltine wrote, 'This is a powerful reason why Westminster should maintain close links with MEPs, and call upon MEPs' knowledge, expertise and power to influence the shape of Community legislation.'[45] Among the suggestions he proposed was to invite British MEPs to be present at meetings of the British Parliament's European Scrutiny Committee. He considered that a second chamber could be introduced into the European Parliament, consisting of members of national parliaments – a 'European Senate'. He recognised that such an innovation would mean a shift of power from national governments to national parliaments but, 'since power has been shifting steadily in the other direction for a long time, this would be no bad thing. Governments should be reminded from time to time that it is not they who are sovereign but Parliament'.[46] He concluded that 'there can be no doubt that the closer the links a national parliament forges with the European Parliament and its committees, the better placed it is to influence in its own national interest'.[47] Sadly, since these recommendations were put forward nearly 30 years ago, he has been proven absolutely correct in his analysis about the growth in the power of the institutions and of the European Parliament in particular.

Strangely, the British political class under Blair and then Cameron invested little time in understanding how the EU institutions worked, not even making significant efforts to ensure that the UK had satisfactory representation in the institutions themselves. Boris Johnson raised this fact during the referendum campaign when he quoted that under 4% of the Eurocrats were of British nationality – not a Brussels problem, more the result of a lack of interest from the UK government side. Furthermore, no time was spent cultivating links of a parliamentary nature across Europe. Quite the contrary. The more the European Parliament grew in activity, power and influence, the less they were prepared to bring British MEPs into British political life.

The European Parliamentary Elections Act in 1999 introduced changes that created large regions, which did not help in retaining contact with individual voters. Instead of having distinct constituencies for individuals to act as parliamentarians, the UK was divided into large regions of which most British citizens found they had little knowledge or understanding. So in the South East, for example, 10 seats were allocated for a total number of voters around 10 million. Proportional representation appeals to many for its ability in theory to treat everyone fairly, but my experience of working with a constituency system first (from 1984 to 1999) and then a proportional one (from 1999 to 2014) made me definitely favour the direct constituency-based link.

One noticeable difference between the UK and other countries which had national list systems was the difference in the nature of parliamentarians. Many continental countries would include in their MEP lists senior former national politicians – such as Leo Tindemans, Belgian Prime Minister from 1974 to 1978 – providing enormous political experience to the European Parliament. Rarely if ever did former senior

UK politicians get selected, not least because of the difficulty of getting selected on the UK's bizarre regional list system.

At least Blair ensured that Labour MEPs had a vote in deciding the leader of the Labour Party along with MPs. Conservatives did not even have that involvement in the party. No frameworks were built within the Conservative Party for MEPs to consult or work with their colleagues in the House of Commons. My experience was that pleasantries were maintained at a local level, but at a national level our knowledge, our experience and our continental friendships counted for nothing.

Worse was that nothing was done at a national level within the House of Commons to keep MPs abreast of developments in European issues. Yes, formal meetings took place at the European Parliament for specific committees, but no provision was made to have either formal or informal links between British MEPs and MPs. Even worse was to come when the passes allowing MEPs access to the two Houses of Parliament were removed between 2004 and 2014 (over the period of two EP mandates). The lack of access made it difficult to maintain friendships with MPs. It was only thanks to the House of Lords, by independent decision, that MEPs retained a means of access to the Houses of Parliament. While the British public might have assumed that MPs and MEPs were working together in their common interest, nothing could have been further from the truth.

Misperceptions of this type have been rife in the UK. However, by all parameters, the European Parliament of elected MEPs has growing powers and is not a sideshow. The fact that since 2009 it has jointly exercised legislative and budgetary functions with the Council of the European Union is significant. It cannot be said to be a mock parliament, as Gove suggested. That attitude is symptomatic of many British politicians who have never made any effort to understand the 'new' institutions in which this country has been involved as an EU member for over 40 years. It simply did not seem to matter to them.

This chapter has documented the lack of attention paid, and even the hostility shown, to providing creative ways to allow MEPs to talk with MPs in the joint interests of their constituents. During the period of our EU membership, the popular press has often taken up issues – real or imaginary – in which the EU has been seen to be intrusive into British lives. Some MPs have been consistently vocal in expressing their resistance to such proposals. The wave of such protest has grown since the Maastricht Treaty was signed. MEPs have had little visible role to play, and national leaders have neither encouraged them to become more visible nor enabled this by including them, even if on several occasions MEPs' actions have helped to maintain British interests. Those with the most publicity were MEPs such as Nigel Farage who were being handsomely paid by the institution they were trying to destroy, but doing little parliamentary work to assist their constituents.

The perceived absence of accountability of the EU institutions struck a strong chord with the British public during the 2016 referendum. However, it was not that this accountability did not exist, but rather that the British political class refused to admit its existence.

3

Future

The first two sections of this pamphlet have been focussed on the Fiction and the Fact in our debates about the relationship between the UK and the EU. Now we turn to the future, reviewing the likely prominent global trends over the next decade. How is the EU likely to react in the light of such trends, and what is at stake should the UK leave the EU as determined by the 2016 referendum?

Setting the scene: key long-term global trends

It may seem strange to write about the next decade, stretching to 2030, when there is such unpredictability about current events in our country, the rest of Europe and the Atlantic alliance. Reliable predictions are increasingly difficult to come by – few were prepared to bet on a Leave vote in the UK referendum, or on the victory of Donald Trump in the US Presidential election in the autumn of 2016. The results of both events are having profound effects, undermining our stability and that of the Western rules-based multilateral global order. The outcome of these upheavals is not yet known.

The ESPAS System

Predicting the future is always a risky business. More often than not, unexpected disruptions occur, upsetting what might have been a logical expectation at the time. A key example of the difficulty of predicting the future with any certainty is the Hudson Institute's report published in the 1960s and looking forward to the year 2000; it failed to foresee the arrival of the microchip, which revolutionised Western society. But we can certainly examine the way in which sectoral trends are developing based on changes underway. In some areas of policy, like demography and the environment, trends are long term in nature, and thus more easily identifiable. In others, such as digital transformation, the speed of change is so fast that predictability is less reliable.

Fortunately, much of what now follows is drawn from the European Strategy and Policy Analysis System (ESPAS), which I helped to found nearly a decade ago. ESPAS has been set up to provide an inter-institutional system at senior EU level to identify medium and long-term trends, as a platform for encouraging strategic thinking and producing common analyses of probable outcomes on major issues for policymakers. In so doing, the system reaches out to academics, think tanks and other stakeholders in order to provide a broad perspective, while developing links with other countries and organisations analysing global trends.

The ESPAS process is coordinated by a steering group chaired by the head of the European Political Strategy Centre (EPSC) in the European Commission. The secretariat of the network is provided by the European Parliament, with senior representatives from the Council of the European Union and the European External Action Service also present. The Committee of the Regions, the Economic and Social Committee and the European Investment Bank sit as observers. ESPAS is the only place in the EU institutions where broader strategic goals can be informally addressed among all the institutions. Attached to the system is a newly introduced open website, the Open Repository Base on International Strategic Studies (ORBIS), which contains relevant information to facilitate citizens' access to information, linking to other websites on long-term trends across the globe.[48] A good example of what can be done with the power of ideas!

Major trends observed in 2010–2019

Foresight is not the art of predicting the future. It is an intellectual exercise in which various alternatives are imagined, enabling a means of shaping the future rather than simply predicting it. Three major exercises carried out by ESPAS over the past decade illustrate how 'mega trends' are developing in major sectors. Firstly, in the spring of 2012, the results of a pilot project were published in which themes such as the empowerment of the individual, the rise of concern about sustainability, an emerging polycentric world and growing gaps in governance were identified as prominent global trends from the present to 2030.[49]

Then, in December 2014, the result of a more thorough exercise was released, confirming these global trends. Three further issues were added to the agenda: the fact that the human race is growing older and richer, with a growing middle class and widening inequalities; a clear shift of economic weight and political power to Asia; and a revolution in technologies and their applications transforming societies in almost every aspect.

To simplify the analysis, three structural revolutions were identified as shaping a more complex and insecure world. First, the economic and technological revolution, where 'the convergence of technologies and the proliferation of tools available to large multitudes will transform economies and societies'. Second, the social and democratic revolution, where 'more empowered and better connected individuals will be more creative, more dynamic, and less wedded to life-time jobs'. Third, the geopolitical revolution, where 'Asia's rise looks set to continue and the roughly two centuries of global dominance by the European continent and the United States are drawing to a close'.[50] As a result of these revolutions:

> The post-war multilateral framework may come under increasing pressure, putting at risk the collective ability to manage increasing interdependence in an efficient manner .... The coming decades are likely to bring growing turbulence and even radical change .... The overall context will be daunting, since the challenges will be interconnected and too big for individual states or even regions to address.[51]

In April 2019, a third report was released, accompanied by think pieces from different EU institutions. These included future analyses on issues such as migration and integration, work and workplaces and urbanisation and megacities.[52]

Major future indicators for policies

By 2030, in general terms, the world will be more numerous, more urban, hotter and more connected. There are four specific central issues which deserve greater attention than others in public debate.

First is the issue of climate change, on which significant work looking to the future has already been published. This is essential to deal with the consequences of past mistakes and prevent future ones. Carbon dioxide that is currently in the atmosphere will remain until around 2060. By 2030, it is estimated that the world will be 1.5 degrees warmer than during pre-industrial times. And should that level be exceeded, more droughts, floods, extreme heat and poverty are expected, as well as more migration. As the latest ESPAS report points out, three actors – China, the US and Europe – are most responsible for the increase in greenhouse gas emissions, due to their sheer size. This challenge can only be met by joint action. Mobilisation, as recently seen on this issue, will be essential to galvanise individual action to reduce such emissions.[53]

Second, the rise of China has instigated a massive shift, which is still underway, in terms of the centre of global economic power, as shown in Table 3. In the early 1800s, before the emergence of the British Empire, China and India had around 50% of global trade. By 1980 that proportion had shrunk to under 6%. But today that percentage of global gross domestic product (GDP) is already over 20%, and is expected to rise to over 35% by 2050.

A valuable book for understanding the implications of this for the West is Kishore Mahbubani's *Has the West Lost It?: A Provocation*. He maintains that a new world order is coming, with China and India as the strongest economies. If the West's two-century epoch as global powerhouse is at an end, what will it do? Mahbubani advises that it is essential for world

Table 3: Percentage share of world GDP to 2050 [54]

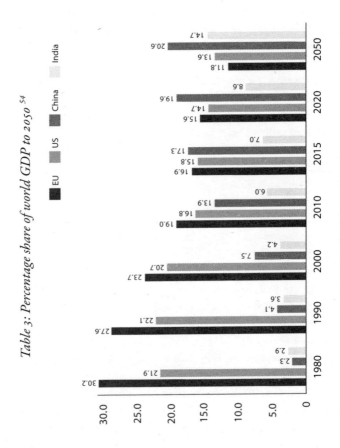

peace that the Western constructs of democracy and reason are part of the new world order, being promoted by diplomacy through multilateral institutions rather than by use of force. Only by recognising its own changing status, and seeking to influence rather than dominate, can the West continue to play a key geopolitical role.

As China rises, it is investing hugely in research and development at a rate which eclipses both the EU and the US. Within five years, China is expected to have a fintech transaction value greater than that of the US. Today, China is home to the world's most valuable artificial intelligence (AI) start-ups. The Made in China 2025 strategy, issued by the Chinese government in 2015, poses an increasing risk of some Western countries becoming vulnerable and succumbing to Chinese pressure (witness the Chinese strategy of recently buying up ports in Greece, Italy and Portugal). More immediately, China is spearheading developments in 5G telecommunications technology that is expected to reshape not only modern economies but modern warfare too. 5G will produce much faster broadband speeds, facilitating initiatives such as driverless cars and advanced automation. In China's five-year plan to 2025, $400 billion is earmarked for 5G-related investments. What is more, Chinese firms could end up holding more than 40% of the standard essential patents for standalone 5G.[55] This issue is well documented in an analysis published in April 2019 by the Mercator Institute for China Studies.[56]

The underlying question is how quickly this growth of economic power will be transformed into military and political influence. China's use of economic power through its Belt and Road Initiative – a strategy of infrastructure investment in dozens of countries to improve intercontinental transport and trade routes – to consolidate its position (potentially enabling military expansion at a later stage) has been documented in detail.[57] The gradual way in which Hong Kong is being subsumed into China, and recent statements by the Chinese President that Taiwan will be a part of China by 2050, are not reassuring.[58] The recent mass demonstrations in Hong Kong about a proposed law on extradition underline the strength of resistance that exists against increasing Chinese influence.

Third, digital transformation now affects all sectors of society. 'The digital economy' has now become 'the economy' in the space of a generation. Digital impacts and disrupts almost everything. The pace of technological change is like a tsunami. The speed of development of new and emerging technologies – such as AI, big data, the internet of things, nanotechnology, quantum computing and 5G – is unknown in human history. They are already causing profound disruption to our economy and to how we interact and communicate. There is a silent revolution towards the 'Knowing Society', which is changing the environment of all our traditional activities, creating new ecosystems, new expectations and new business models. The Knowing Society is a world in which, thanks to connectivity and digital transformation, almost all can be found out. Going forward, we can either ride the wave and adjust existing businesses to emerging technologies, or ignore technological trends. An emerging digital-driven economy will involve huge transferences of data across the confines of geographies and the limits of traditional boundaries. As the saying goes, you can draw a line in the sand, but it is hard to draw a line in the cloud. In a digital society, automation will become far more

pervasive as machines exchange data with each other. Reskill-
ing and labour market transition will become of great signifi-
cance, since most tasks have the potential to be automated.[59]
Finally, in politics, the impact of technologies on democratic
structures is increasingly transformative. With the decen-
tralisation of power and information control, new actors
are exploiting developments to undermine faith and trust
in Western democracies. The Russian Minister of Defence
Sergei Shoigu was quoted as saying in 2015, 'The day has come
when we all have to admit that a word, a camera, a photo, the
Internet, and information in general have become yet another
type of weapons [sic], yet another component of the armed
forces.'[60]

Fourth, the multilateral order is now more fragile than in
the past. Globalisation and digitalisation have, as previously
noted, essentially shaped the way in which the world has
modernised over the past three decades. Recently, however,
the character and tempo of globalisation have changed. The
pace of economic integration has slowed down, leading to
'slowbalisation' (a term coined by the Dutch trendwatcher
Adjiedj Bakas to describe the reaction against globalisation).[61]
In January 2019, *The Economist* analysed the phenomenon's
severity and what commerce will look like in its aftermath:

Viewed in the very long run, over centuries, the march of
globalisation is inevitable, barring an unforeseen catas-
trophe. Technology advances, lowering the cost of trade
in every corner of the world, while the human impulse
to learn, copy and profit from strangers is irrepressible.
Yet there can be long periods of slowbalisation, when

integration stagnates or declines. The golden age of globalisation created huge benefits but also costs and a political backlash. The new pattern of commerce that replaces it will be no less fraught with opportunity and danger.[62]

There are those who are determined not to let the rules-based multilateral order disappear without a fight. A speech by the German Chancellor, Angela Merkel, at the 2019 Munich Security Conference provoked the following comment from Ulrich Speck, writing for the German Marshall Fund of the United States:

> Russia and China act along the lines of great-power competition, and use the liberal international order only as instruments to achieve their direct interests in this context, considering rules and institutions only as a means to constrain others and increase their own power. While under Obama the United States acted as a counterbalance to this transactional view of international order, the Trump administration has at least partly joined Russia and China in such a view of international rules and institutions.[63]

I believe that it is not the time to give up on the future of an effective and close transatlantic partnership, even if it does not look good with the current US administration. We should listen to those like US senator Bob Menendez, who called for a strengthened US–Europe alliance while speaking in Brussels in February 2019. He said, 'In a world where we need to work together to face real threats, I for one humbly believe that the US should lecture less and lead more.'[64] James Kynge, an expert on China, has also emphasised the importance of alliances, quoting the Chinese academic Yan Zuetong:

> 'We are moving away from a state in which international norms are led by Western liberalism to a state where international norms are no longer respected.' Without norms of behaviour, countries may find that their only option is to cleave to those with power – and that will ultimately mean choosing between the US and China.[65]

Overall, analysing changing global trends allows policy-makers to have better control over their destiny, shaping their future. The hope of the ESPAS project is to empower European leaders to see where policy choices are heading; in order to avoid the occurrence tomorrow of undesirable outcomes, those policies should be altered today.

How will the EU shape up to future challenges?

After the Great Recession and the massive migration crisis in 2015/16, as well as the UK's decision in June 2016 to withdraw from the EU, it is not surprising that the EU has principally focussed on making the system work effectively, rather than on what its priorities should be in 2030. Three different avenues are open to EU policy-makers.

An ambitious, forward-looking approach

Major speeches have been made since the 2016 referendum by European leaders – such as German Chancellor Angela Merkel, European Commission President Jean-Claude Juncker and French President Emmanuel Macron – setting out an overall direction for the EU to follow. There is a high degree of overlap and convergence between them, both in terms of the visions outlined and specific initiatives proposed.

All three leaders share concerns over Europe's long-term prospects; a desire to shape Europe's future; an ambition to strengthen Europe's unique value proposition at home and abroad; and a focus on action and delivery. They differ on the question of timing for delivery, Macron presenting a two-stage time frame centred first on the European Parliament elections of May 2019 and then the following elections running in 2024. They also differ in their methods. While the overriding concern of Juncker is the unity of the EU, Macron calls for more differentiated and flexible institutional arrangements to support his visions, including enabling member states to do more, if they would like. While the Merkel and Juncker changes can be implemented without treaty change, some of those recommended by Macron would require treaty change. He is not reluctant to expound the idea that it is helpful to promote collective EU action, through the concept of European rather than national sovereignty, to protect European citizens' interests in the face of rising authoritarianism.[66] His argument is that by pooling at EU level, nations actually increase their sovereignty by strengthening their ability to act in ways conducive with their national interest and to project it on the global stage.

As the summary document comparing these approaches reveals, 'while President Juncker wants to fix Europe's roof "now that the sun is shining", President Macron outlines a vision on how to rebuild the European House'.[67] The three leaders, for example, all call for an effective European border police force, since common borders require common protection. There is also significant convergence on trade and multi-lateralism to help shape fairer, more inclusive globalisation, as well as the need to better protect and project European interests and values in global markets. They also share the objective of a more democratic union.

In January 2019, Merkel and Macron signed a new treaty – the Aachen Treaty – pledging to coordinate policy on the 56th anniversary of the 1963 Élysée Treaty, an accord of friendship and reconciliation between their two counties. In the current difficult European political environment, this illustrates that their joint priorities lie more in strengthening foreign and defence cooperation than in measures to deepen economic and monetary union. Steps are being taken in the right direction to underpin the European capacity to act.[68]

President Macron made a speech on 10th May 2019, prior to the European Parliament elections, to chart the road to European renewal, building on the pillars of freedom, protection and progress:

> We cannot let nationalists without solutions exploit the people's anger. We cannot sleepwalk through a diminished Europe. We cannot become ensconced in business as usual and wishful thinking. European humanism demands action. And everywhere, the people are standing up to be part of that change.[69]

Then, in June 2019, the European Council agreed a new Strategic Agenda for 2019–2024, providing an overall framework and direction to guide the work of the institutions over the next five years, including most of the policy priorities set out in the discussion of global trends earlier in this chapter. This has now been complemented by a detailed five-year policy agenda from the incoming President of the European Commission, Ursula von der Leyen, which was presented during the debates for her approval by the European Parliament in July 2019.

A minimalist, populist approach

The visions set out by Merkel, Juncker and Macron are of course targets for the EU to aspire to over the coming decade. But there are more immediate threats to the stability of the EU that must be confronted – not least the rise of populism across the continent, fuelled by adverse economic conditions under which incomes have been stagnant for nearly a decade, and the arrival of migrants, who have travelled in considerable numbers to some parts of the EU. The political scientist Matthew Goodwin put it bluntly:

> Since the vote for Brexit ... populist forces have gained momentum across the EU [in countries such as] Austria, Germany, Italy or Sweden .... The EU faces serious challenges on multiple fronts .... Jarring values and contrasting identities demarcate East and West; North and South are, economically, different planets; there is still no unified response to the refugee crisis; nor any coherent strategy for budget reform and boosting productivity in response to ageing and depopulating societies.[70]

In reviewing *National Populism: The Revolt Against Liberal*

Democracy, the book Goodwin co-authored with Roger Eatwell, *The Economist* warned of revolts to come:

> Brexit or no Brexit, nationalist populism will be an important part of British politics for decades. Many feel the odds are stacked against them. The post-industrial economy combines large amounts of disruption with slow growth .... Brexit is an example of what can happen if politicians refuse to deal with popular fears about emotive subjects before they become toxic.[71]

In advance of the elections in May 2019, there were real fears of the European Parliament being swamped by a tide of populist representatives, under the orchestration of Steve Bannon and powered by the Italian firebrand politician Matteo Salvini. In an effort to make their policies more appealing to a wider electorate, right-wing parties such as Marine Le Pen's National Rally toned down their rhetoric for their countries to leave the EU. Most notably, the Italian Prime Minister, Giuseppe Conte, said Italy has no chance to leave the EU as the country wants to confront its problems from the inside.[72]

And yet, when the results came in, not only did turnout exceed 50%, rising by 9% compared to the last election in 2014, but the greatest gains went to the Liberal and Green political groups, increasing their representation by a combined 60 seats. By contrast, the far-right and nationalist anti-EU groups increased their representation by 22 seats.[73] So the question of how great a political force populism will represent in the decade ahead will greatly depend on how the EU handles its policy priorities.

A pragmatic appraisal

The continuing decline of the two major political groups of the European Parliament in the 2019 European election was to be expected. But the substantial increase in turnout after more than two decades of gradual reduction was a great surprise, not least to members of the Anglo-Saxon press, who had to explain to their readers that the expected takeover of the European Parliament by the populist groups had not taken place as forecast. The fact that the Liberal (subsequently renamed Renew Europe) and Green groups benefitted most is a sign that strong campaigning on ideas for action is the best means to defeat the destructive populist rhetoric.

What many Eurosceptics, including many in the UK, underestimate is the remarkable resilience of the EU system. There have been times over the past decade when it has looked as if the EU could fragment, not least in relation to the Great Recession and the huge strains that it placed on the euro. Mario Draghi, President of the European Central Bank (ECB), showed his determination to ensure that all would be well in an exemplary manner, saying in 2012, 'The ECB is ready to do whatever it takes to preserve the euro.'[74] Thus, while the EU has been gradually coming out of recession and austerity, the EU system has continued to function and has not ceased to adapt, for example with progress being made towards a European banking union enabling better banking supervision. A recent document submitted by the Commission to the May European Council meeting showed that 75% of citizens living in the euro area are in favour of the euro – the highest level since the introduction of the currency. Polling for the Eurobarometer in spring 2019 showed that support for the EU among its citizens is at its highest level since 1983. Sometimes, it is evident that processes are so slow that Europeans do not see that progress is taking place. But an interesting phrase attributed to Galileo, insisting that the Earth revolves round the sun despite the claims of his critics, is relevant here: *'eppur si muove'* – 'and yet it moves'! The EU does indeed move, albeit slowly!

The EU has continued to legislate, although less than in the past. One example loved by some and disliked by others is the GDPR, which came into force in May 2018. This was a piece of legislation subject to over 3,000 amendments in the European Parliament, which provided heated debate on key questions of data privacy. In retrospect, with the significant disruption caused by the Cambridge Analytica affair – in which millions of profiles from a Facebook database were misused and militarised for political purposes – such a significant step has been broadly welcomed. In October 2018, the heads of Apple and Facebook 'called on the US government to adopt tough EU-style privacy laws, challenging White House objections that European regulation is imposing red tape on American technology businesses'.[75] This is a clear example showing that where the EU takes the lead, others can follow – and it shows that those who said transatlantic cooperation has ground to a halt are mistaken.

While the UK has been absorbed by the Brexit debate, the EU has surprisingly made progress in pursuing an active multilateral agenda. Following the successful signature of the Comprehensive Economic and Trade Agreement (CETA) deal with Canada, further bilateral agreements have been concluded with Mercosur and signed with Singapore and

Vietnam, while that with Japan has already entered into force. The EU has also reached political agreement on updating its bilateral deal with Mexico, and continues to negotiate with countries such as Australia, New Zealand and Indonesia.

In line with history, the EU has taken its biggest leaps when faced with substantial changes in its surrounding environment. So it was with the Maastricht Treaty following the collapse of the Soviet Union in 1990, or before the accession to the EU of ten countries from Central and Eastern Europe. Looking at the previously mentioned indicators of global trends, the three following examples show how the EU's progress towards greater cooperation over the next decade will be accelerated by outside pressures from China, Russia and Africa.

First, the rise of China requires an innovative response. Not all Western leaders are yet convinced that China presents a real challenge for Europe, considering its influence benign. But as time passes, China's growing dominance in the domain of technology will mobilise the EU, along with the US, to assess what should be done to avoid China beginning to set global standards for such issues as 5G. The West should take major initiatives to invest in joint schemes to develop technologies together. Specifically, a recent McKinsey report, identifying Europe's digital gap, recommended prioritising five areas to accelerate the path to AI.[76] It is very unlikely that sanctioning trade tariffs against China will be enough to resolve the IT issue alone. We will come to realise that, whatever nice words the Chinese have to support the multilateral system, they are thinking of China first. Indeed, the EU has recently designated China as a 'systemic rival'. The current sensitivity about the participation of Huawei in the European rollout of 5G shows the dilemma clearly. Indeed, this is likely to be the first of many such issues, with AI, big data and battery technology all likely to form the nucleus of a technological rivalry.

Second, the military might of Russia will concentrate European minds to do more in the field of arms procurement, building a European army together. This is presaged in the Aachen Treaty, which states, 'The two countries undertake to continue to intensify the cooperation between their armed forces with a view to the establishment of a common culture and joint deployments. They shall intensify the development of common defence programmes.'[77]

Third is the question relating to migration and demography. Looking at 2030, Europeans will represent a smaller proportion of the world population (they accounted for 25% in 1900 compared to a projected 5% in 2060), and will be much older than their more youthful neighbours in Africa and Asia.[78] These latter fast-growing populations will be more willing to move, living in areas which are more politically unstable than Europe. Such pressures will encourage Europeans to take joint action on strengthening their external border. The spread of digitalisation is a game changer, heightening aspirations, while issues regarding lifelong learning and retirement ages are relevant for Europeans.

It would certainly be useful if the EU could better integrate some strategic capacity for policy-making that is more effective than that which exists today. In a recent article in the *Berlin Policy Journal*, looking at the 2040 horizon, a scenario was forecast in which, owing to external pressures, Europe got lucky and evolved into a guarantor of regional and global stability.[79] As part of that imagined development, a truly Europe-wide direct election of the President of the European Commission was held in 2029. Such a development would be facilitated if the EU could manage to complete the single market over the next decade. It is estimated that the 'cost of non-Europe' in principal policy areas is around €2 trillion.[80]

Pressures will also come internally for reform of the EU institutions. Earlier in this book, I drew a comparison between the US and the EU, both being structures where the executive is separated from the legislature. In historical terms, it is noticeable that the US made several amendments to its constitution in the early days, from 1791 to 1804. Similarly, the EU has made amendments to the Treaty of Rome, mostly within the last 30 years. At present, there is no real pressure for amending the treaties to strengthen EU powers as there was following the fall of the Berlin Wall in 1989. The mood is much more suited to consolidating the powers that the EU has, using existing treaties as the bases for joint actions. So incremental progress can be expected.

The incoming President of the European Commission made it clear in her speech to the European Parliament in July 2019 that she intends to make a new push for European democracy. This includes improving the lead candidate, or 'Spitzenkandidaten', process. This is a procedure whereby European political parties appoint lead candidates to become European Commission President, ahead of European elections. This role is then given to the candidate whose political party marshalls sufficient parliamentary support. The European Parliament has wanted to ensure that, by voting in European elections, Europeans citizens not only elect the European Parliament itself but also have a say over who heads the European Commission. This process first operated in 2014, when Juncker was chosen to head the European Commission, being selected as the candidate of the lead party, and then nominated by the European Council. David Cameron failed to understand this change when he tried to block the nomination of Juncker in 2014, together with Viktor Orbán, the Hungarian Prime Minister; it was not in his power to do so! In July 2019, the final choice of European Commission President did not come from a Spitzenkandidat, as there was no agreement within the European Council to follow this process. But, in the decade ahead, it is to be expected that this system will be developed, possibly along with the idea of transnational lists for European Parliament elections. As this democratisation process unfurls, consideration should be given to allowing national parliaments to have greater involvement in the accountability of EU institutions through revising the provisions of the National Parliament Protocol attached to the Lisbon Treaty (see Chapter 2).

Nevertheless, as the focus of political parties will be on connecting with their voters to head off the populist wave, and helping provide them with economic and political security, so will pressures rise over the decade ahead for steps to be taken towards EU reform, no doubt encouraged by the need to adapt the treaties to allow the EU to be more effective in certain areas of policy action, such as the development of an EU army. Macron's views about the evolution of the EU were reflected in a recent supplement to *The Economist* putting forward the case for flexibility. It expressed the view that the EU must embrace greater differentiation through 'a true multi-speed, multi-tier Europe' based around the idea of 'variable geometry', or face potential disintegration.[81] The central core would be the 19-member euro zone, surrounded by a second tier containing the EU members who are not euro members. A third tier would consist of those countries who want to participate as much as possible in the single market, but not become EU members. A final tier would contain those countries who would like to have a comprehensive trade agreement with the EU, but not to accept its rules.[82]

Although some think that the UK's withdrawal will seriously impair the EU's ability to function effectively, I subscribe to the view that it is more likely to allow the EU to develop faster and further than it would have done if the UK were still a member, as Clare Foges has argued in *The Times*.[83] Oddly enough, however, should the previously mentioned suggestion by *The Economist* take shape, this would provide an opportunity for the UK to connect with the EU in a different manner.

Despite there being massive challenges ahead for the EU, there is a very good chance that, slowly but surely, it will resolve its difficulties in the knowledge that if it does not, Europe risks returning to a scenario of competing nation states trying to solve global challenges, including relationships with the UK – which would not be in the overall interests of Europeans.

Long-term trends: the UK dimension

At the time of writing, in the summer of 2019, we find ourselves in the unexpected situation of having negotiated with the EU a withdrawal agreement which is legally enforceable but incapable of finding the support of a majority in the House of Commons. This is accompanied by a non-binding political declaration setting out ideas for a future UK–EU trade deal to be completed once the withdrawal agreement is approved. The paramount driving force today is to resolve the Brexit dilemma as soon as possible. Three points of fundamental importance can be noted from the Brexit negotiations so far.

First, observers were struck by the British negotiators' great expectation from the outset that everything could be resolved rapidly, unravelling more than 40 years' worth of European regulation within the space of a couple of years. It was a common expectation that everything could be wrapped up, including a trade deal, before our planned departure at the end of March 2019, with a transition period of a maximum of a couple of years to implement the decisions agreed.

The fact that this objective was never going to be achievable, as the trade agreement could only be signed once the UK had left the EU, did not seem to occur to the British negotiators (one of whom admitted candidly that he had not realised the depth of the problems that leaving the EU would cause).[84] The Brexiteer MEP Daniel Hannan reflected an optimistic view when he wrote in glowing terms that the prospects for the UK outside the EU were unbeatable:

> The strongest case for leaving is that it offers a better future. Not just a safer future. Not just a more democratic future. Not just a future where Britain's pride, confidence and global links are restored. We'd be better off in the literal, financial sense .... It's 2020, and the UK is flourishing outside of the EU. The rump Union, now a united

bloc, continues its genteel decline, but Britain has become the most successful and competitive knowledge-based economy in the region.[85]

A more realistic assessment of the post-Brexit position of the UK was set out by Boris Johnson in a *Telegraph* article in 2013:

> If we left the EU, we would end this sterile debate, and we would have to recognise that most of our problems are not caused by "Bwussels", but by chronic British short-termism, inadequate management, sloth, low skills, a culture of easy gratification and under-investment in both human and physical capital and infrastructure. Why are we still, person for person, so much less productive than the Germans? That is now a question more than a century old, and the answer has nothing to do with the EU. In or out of the EU, we must have a clear vision of how we are going to be competitive in a global economy.[86]

Second, once the referendum result was announced and May became Prime Minister, the guidelines for the departure of the UK were set out in her speech to the Conservative Party conference in October 2016. It was music to the ears of hard-line Brexiteers. The four principles for Brexit became: no single market, no customs union, no European Court of Justice influence and no huge payments to the EU after departure. May's Lancaster House speech in January 2017 also included a commitment to no hard border between the Republic of Ireland and Northern Ireland. At this early stage, a more pragmatic approach would have been to follow the detailed 'Flexcit' recommendations put forward by the Leave Alliance, whose proposal document (running to over 400 pages) advocated a gradual withdrawal from the EU.[87]

It seems to have been difficult for British political negotiators to take into account that if they had red lines, then so did others. The EU has made very clear from the outset of the talks following the referendum that its red line was that the single market and its four freedoms would remain indivisible. Quentin Peel put it concisely:

> Theresa May and her advisers have always overestimated the room for manoeuvre in the German government, and their willingness to compromise on fundamental principles of the EU single market and the legal authority of EU institutions like the European Court of Justice .... The idea that the UK can stay in a customs union for goods but not for services, while not accepting freedom of movement, is regarded in Germany not merely as "cherry-picking" but as blatantly "unfair". The integrity of the single market is seen as essential to preserve a level playing-field between competitors, as well as to protect the fundamental cohesion of the EU. It is a moral question, as much as an economic one.[88]

The EU was expected to give way once the House of Commons had passed a resolution or the Brady amendment in early 2019. The reality was, and will be, that the EU would not tear up its rule book to suit one member state, about to become a third country. It is not a question of wanting to punish Britain, more a question of survival for the EU.

Third, looking at the global trends outlined earlier in this chapter, we are moving into an era where, if we are to effectively deal with challenges ahead, more European action – not less – will be needed, for example to maintain the multilateral trading system or to take collective action on climate change. Regional blocs will continue to be the building blocks of the international trading system, with decisions being taken by the four major trade negotiators – the US, the EU, China and Russia. The belief that the UK can have greater influence outside the EU than within it is delusional. Globalisation and digital transformation mean that the supply chains of the business world have become more complex, and large multinationals have much more open choice about where to invest than beforehand. As a result, since June 2016, major multinationals have announced intentions to move their headquarters to the continent in order to be covered by EU rules. These companies include many in the financial sector, as well as Panasonic and Sony, with car producers like Honda, Nissan and BMW hedging their bets by limiting production. And although the inventor James Dyson, a prominent supporter of Brexit, had access to UK research funds to develop his new electric car, he decided that his new factory would be built in Singapore to be close to the Asian market, in particular China.

The vital role of youth in the future of the UK

One of the strongest campaign slogans for the Leavers was the idea that we would shape a global Britain, seeking to recreate the concept of the Anglosphere, linking with our long-lost friends such as the Australians and Canadians. This was evidenced, or so it was claimed, by the fact that the EU was declining, having the lowest growth rate in the Western world and no future prospects. A tantalising vision was set out, supposedly inspiring us all to think of a myriad array of countries where there were new markets for the taking – the shackles of Brussels only had to be shed and everything would be OK. But there is disquieting news to be inferred from Table 3. It shows that Western countries, not just in the EU but also the US, are declining in terms of their percentage of world GDP, compared to the rise of India and China. Furthermore, all data available from the referendum has shown that Brexit was a concept appealing more to older generations who were more familiar with the Commonwealth than the younger ones.

The BBC published a revealing article in September 2018. It examined the referendum result and found:

> Studies suggest just over 70% of 18–24 year-olds voted Remain, while just under 30% opted to vote Leave .... So, it's fair to say that on the whole, younger people were more pro-EU than their parents and grandparents – only 40% of those aged 65 and over supported Remain .... In a nutshell, the UK is currently divided into the under-45s who, broadly, are in favour of staying in the EU, and the over-45s, who largely want out.[89]

The question of Brexit and the British was superbly assessed by Stephen Green in his book *Brexit and the British: Who Are We Now?*. He points out that few voices from the Remain side were prepared to argue their case in terms of a European identity. Why? The truth, Green says, is that British identity is still deeply imbued with its imperial past:

Through all the imperial diversions and distractions of the two and a half centuries during which Britain has nurtured its identity, it has consistently had to be reminded that it is also European by virtue of geographical and cultural realities we cannot deny .... If we pretend that we can ignore this element of our identity, that we are just a member of the global community of nations, and that trading with the world is the be-all and end-all of a robust national identity, then we deceive ourselves about our own roots, and about who we really are. There is a profound threat to our identity in the way post-Brexit Britain proposes to present itself as 'Global Britain' .... At every stage of the intellectual life of Europe, people from this country have played leading roles .... This European conversation was, and remains, an essential part of the British spirit and of the British identity. We share so much more with the other Europeans than just geography: there are deep cultural continuities we cannot deny without denying our history and impoverishing ourselves.[90]

In time, the younger generation will come to understand that the referendum result of 2016 was a great mistake for our country, and will no doubt wish to rectify the decision which could effectively deprive them of their European citizenship. Realising that it is better to be globalists with a European base, they will make their views known through such vehicles as the Ideas Network 2030 (IN2030), a newly launched online think tank welcoming young ideas-driven participants from the centre right of British politics.

The UK–EU relationship: a way ahead

Taking into account the previous observations about the need for close cooperation with the EU for enhancement of our national interests and for giving our young generation a wider sense of international action through remaining close to the EU and involved in its activities, the most logical choice would have been for the government, with the support of parliament, to opt for a phased withdrawal as recommended by the Leave Alliance, maintaining membership of the European Free Trade Association (EFTA) for a reasonable period of time as new arrangements were put in place. But emotions are taking precedence over common sense.

It is noticeable that the tone of debate has distinctly hardened since the 2016 referendum, at which time many Brexiteers were openly recommending a Norway-style deal looking for association with the EU after the departure of the UK. Now recent polls have shown that the majority of Conservative members openly support a no-deal option, indicating that they have been persuaded that this course of action will not involve major economic dislocation. Many of those who voted Leave will be the hardest hit. 'Do not believe in experts' seems to be the cry, when all evidence from government sources illustrates that an exit of this kind would bring huge economic upheaval to Britain, not least because there would then be no transitional period during which businesses could adjust. A letter in *The Times* from John Neill, CEO of Unipart, warned of the threat to the British automotive industry, which employs more than 800,000 people, should frictionless trade and regulatory alignment with Europe be removed.[91]

Christopher Booker has warned about the risks of taking

such a hard line and in effect making Britain what the EU terms a 'third country':

> By ripping us out of the incredibly complex system that had so tightly integrated our economy with the rest of the EU, we were putting at risk not just a large part of our currently 'frictionless' export trade with the EU itself, which provides an eighth of our national income. We were also risking much of our trade with other countries across the world, which is currently conducted under trade deals negotiated between those countries and the EU.[92]

Current suggestions for a managed no-deal to take place using Article 24 of the General Agreement on Tariffs and Trade (GATT) have been proven to be built on sand, and in any case dependent on the EU playing ball. A recent leading article in *The Times* summed it up nicely, saying, 'Too many senior Tories have for too long been too scared to tell the public the truth about no-deal.'[93] That edition of the newspaper went on to indicate that the most detailed government estimate concluded that a Brexit scenario falling back on World Trade Organization rules would cut GDP growth in Britain by about eight percentage points over the next 15 years when compared to a benchmark of continued EU membership.

With the meeting between the new UK government team and Commission representatives expected in the early autumn of 2019, there can be little room for optimism that a deal will be struck by 31 October. Not only is it unlikely that there will be anyone in Brussels with whom to negotiate, but also the EU has made it crystal clear that the withdrawal

agreement cannot be reopened. (The only possibility of alter-
ing the content of the withdrawal agreement would be if the
British government decided to change its red lines; there is
little chance of that happening under current circumstances.)
Moreover, suggestions of withholding the financial settlement
as leverage to secure changes to EU negotiating principles
would be in effect illegal.

A way in which the withdrawal agreement package might
pass through the House of Commons would be if changes were
made to the non-binding political declaration to bring greater
clarity on what the future trading deal might look like. But as
it stands today, in the words of Ivan Rogers, the UK's former
Ambassador to the EU, the political declaration is 'vague to
the point of vacuity .... Any number of different final destina-
tions are accommodable within this text'.[94] The UK will have
to choose eventually between remaining in a customs union
– for reasons of the backstop (to avoid a hard Irish border) as
well as to ensure frictionless trade to keep half of our exports
going to the EU – or reaching a free-trade agreement like
those that the EU has with Canada and Japan, which would
not give frictionless access for our exports or solve the Irish
border question. It is difficult to see a majority for reconcil-
ing a customs union approach as favoured by Labour, with a
trade agreement broadly favoured by right-wing Conservatives. Furthermore, it is difficult to see long-term support for
remaining in limbo, being part of a customs union but having
no say on the EU rules which apply to the UK.

(It should be remembered that before the withdrawal
agreement can come into force, the European Parliament
will have to give its consent – the bête noire of Michael Gove

– paving the way for years of negotiations between the EU and the UK on what should be included in such a trade deal.)

As all these points are taken on board, we will realise that the unashamed optimism of the Brexiteer MEP Daniel Hannan was once again misplaced. In 2016 he shared his vision of Britain outside the EU, writing as if looking back on events from an imagined future:

> Once outside the Common External Tariff, the UK swiftly signed a slew of free-trade agreements, including with the US, India and Australia. Our policy is like Switzerland's: we match EU trade negotiators when convenient, but go further when Brussels is reluctant to liberalise, as with China. Following Switzerland, we forged overseas relationships while remaining full members of the EU's common market – covered by free movement of goods, services and capital.[95]

Predictions like this will be proven to be totally misleading, as the people behind them always believed they could have their cake and eat it. The trouble was that they never understood that the Swiss version of an economic relationship would not be on offer to the UK. Boris Johnson was contemptuous, saying 'f—k business' when asked about business leaders' fears about Brexit. It is still evident that many Brexiteers believe that, in the end, the EU will sacrifice political principle over economic considerations. They are sadly mistaken.

Thus we are really between a rock and a hard place. The choice is between a totally irresponsible no-deal option or a deal which will leave us economically worse off than before.

An interesting recent article by a highly respected Brexiteer, Peter Oborne, called for us to swallow our pride and think again, taking a long extension to reflect how best to proceed.[96] Given that there is no valid case to say that we will be better off with Brexit, and that the withdrawal agreement is simply going to usher in years of wrangling about our relationship with the EU, it is not surprising that pressures have risen to have either a general election or a second referendum. My preference would be the latter.

Thinking of the interests of the UK, not least for its ability to best look after its citizens in the years ahead, as well as of its young generation, among whom many fulminate about an older generation depriving them of their European citizenship, we will have to revisit the need to consult voters once again as to whether they want the kind of deal that has been negotiated on their behalf. The People's Vote campaign is strongly advocating for this to happen. Of the various versions of a new referendum proposed, the best, as suggested by the MP Justine Greening, would have three options open to voters, who would eliminate them on a preferential basis: deal, no-deal or no Brexit.

In any future referendum, rather than circulating economic fear sheets about leaving the EU, it is essential to explain to the public in simple terms what the EU institutions are, how they work and what influence they have on the daily lives of British people. Pre-internet, it might have been possible to push this information under the carpet, but in today's world, that is totally unacceptable. It should be carefully explained that the purpose of the EU is to provide stability through shared institutions and policies to ensure the freedom and prosperity of its peoples. What was truly shocking in the debates of the referendum campaign was the insouciance of many Brexiteers who argued that it would be easy to leave the EU, not realising that literally thousands of pieces of legislation created under the EU framework were applicable to the UK and could not be wound up overnight. Remainers were complacent, anticipating an easy victory, and they never adequately explained the idea of shared sovereignty. The fact that Germany was prepared to share its sovereignty to make Europe a better place should have been promoted more widely to show that our policy dilemmas – such as issues relating to the environment – would be more easily resolved through a European solution.

A further consultation of the British people is not easy to set in motion. But given that there is no other satisfactory option, and that we have had three meaningful votes in the House of Commons, it is entirely justifiable to undertake a further consultation of the British public on the outcome of a deal, now that more than three years have passed since the original referendum.

Birds have come home to roost. Long-term global trends indicate the emergence of a very different world to the one we have known, where old certainties fade away to be replaced by unpredictable events. Thus the way in which the EU is putting forward ideas for the next decade has some semblance of credibility. What gives rise to concern for the UK is the lack of long-term thinking as to what will happen once we are out of the EU. Can we really depend on new trade deals from other countries to give us the same levels of employment and prosperity? How many leading companies and banks are departing the UK, since we cannot give them the certainty required for long-term investment?

The lack of knowledge of the EU, its policies and its institutions showed up at every stage in the negotiation process for the withdrawal agreement. Will the same be true for the next crucial stage of negotiations for the UK–EU trade agreement? Above all, a young generation, who mostly voted for Remain, will feel that they have lost a part of their being along with the loss of their EU citizenship. They must be consulted on the deal that is finally struck, as it is they who will have to live with the consequences of a more limited outlook for their future lives and careers.

4

Conclusions

An irrefutable fact of our era is that we are living through a technological revolution which is nowhere near finished. Another is that economic power is continuing to shift across the globe to China and Asia. In the 1950s, the economic centre of the world was on the Eastern seaboard of the US; by 2030, it will be somewhere near China, close to where it used to be at the turn of the 19th century. It is not just the continental European powers which are in proportionate decline, but also the US and the UK too. The technological revolution is like a tsunami, accelerating our ability to connect across the globe and generating unimaginable changes through digital trans- formation, with the availability of data, as well as automation, changing the nature of the work in which we are involved. As a result, globalisation accelerates, meaning that more rather than less action is required at European level to tackle issues such as climate change.

In a stimulating comparison, Ian Goldin and Chris Kutarna compare our era to the Renaissance. As in that time, when jobs were threatened and conspicuous inequality existed, so today information revolutions do not allow only good ideas to flour- ish – they also provide a platform for dangerous ideas. The Zuckerberg information revolution can pose a similar threat to that of Gutenberg. Goldin and Kutarna plead for progress to prevail through evidence-based, innovative and reasoned thinking.[97]

Over the past 30 years, fundamental changes have occurred to the EU treaties through which the EU has direct and indirect accountability to European voters, although it falls some way short of a 'Federal States of Europe'. The British political world has been slow to adapt, in terms of the policies introduced into EU law as well as the increases in the powers of the EU institutions, in particular the European Parliament. British politicians have shown reluctance in explaining the decisions they have taken, not telling the British people about the changes to which they have agreed. They still do not do this even when a referendum is called, leaving voters in the dark as to who is responsible for what and not explaining the democratic accountability which exists.

The referendum called by Cameron, ostensibly to resolve the splits in the Conservative Party over Europe, should never have been called at the time chosen by the former Prime Minister, as other member states were incapable at that time of opening up the treaties for revision, owing to their slow recovery from the Great Recession of 2009. Furthermore, their attention was totally absorbed by the major migration crisis on their hands across the Mediterranean. Nor should any commitment have been given by the former Prime Minister to accept that an advisory referendum be taken to be obligatory, thus undermining the principle that parliament is sovereign.

Should we leave the EU, we will realise in time that the deal we had, a bespoke arrangement within the EU – not being a member of the euro or the borderless Schengen Area – was our best option, as we had a seat at the table with our elected representatives giving voice to our concerns. The Brexit negotiations have shown that not understanding the EU institutions and its policies, and overestimating the EU's will to make exceptions for the UK in its future trading relationship, have been real drawbacks for long-term British interests. With luck, we will avoid a rupture – a no-deal scenario – which would be catastrophic for the UK as well as the EU. Instead, hopefully, we will keep our sanity and have a second vote. Then a younger generation will find the determination to explain what the real, rather than imaginary, challenges are for Britain over the years ahead. In so doing, they will ensure that the future for the British tomorrow will indeed be a global one, but with a European base.

Endnotes

1   Simon Nixon, 'If Britain is to win a deal on Brexit it
     must learn the EU's language', *The Times*, 28th June
     2018, https://www.thetimes.co.uk/article/if-britain-
     is-to-win-a-deal-on-brexit-it-must-learn-the-eu-s-
     language-sbfsvxpxm, accessed 3rd April 2019.
2   Nixon, 'If Britain is to win'.
3   Quoted by Lord Privy Seal Francis Pakenham,
     HL deb, 2nd May 1967, vol. 282, col. 846, https://
     hansard.parliament.uk/Lords/1967-05-02/
     debates/1c60b4f6-2cb6-42e6-8906-0aa8b2b7a019/
     TheEuropeanEconomicCommunityBritishApplication,
     accessed 3rd April 2019.
4   Edward Heath, 'Message from the Prime Minister', *The
     Illustrated London News*, January 1973.
5   HC deb, 26th October 1971, vol. 823, col. 1634,
     https://hansard.parliament.uk/Commons/1971-10-
     26/debates/d4128899-e9f2-48b5-b300-8aae13199d7f/
     EuropeanCommunities, accessed 3rd April 2019.
6   HC deb, 28th October 1971, vol. 823, col. 2210,
     https://hansard.parliament.uk/Commons/1971-10-
     28/debates/f7b49d76-2531-4c3e-9af3-bf15653b73f7/
     EuropeanCommunities, accessed 3rd April 2019.
7   Greg Rosen, 'No, Britain wasn't lied to when we joined
     the EU. We knew what we were getting into', *The*

Telegraph, 29th March 2016, https://www.telegraph.
co.uk/opinion/2016/03/29/no-britain-wasnt-lied-to-
when-we-joined-the-eu-we-knew-what-we-w, accessed
3rd April 2019.

8   Quoted in Michael Cockerell, 'How Britain first fell for
Europe', *BBC*, 4th June 2005, http://news.bbc.co.uk/1/
hi/uk/4609131.stm, accessed 3rd April 2019.

9   Margaret Thatcher, '5 Firm Reasons for Voting "Yes to
Europe"', *Yes to Europe: Conservative Campaign Notes*,
no. 6, 2nd June 1975.

10   Quoted in Dawn Sellars, 'The 1975 Referendum on
Europe', *Oxpol*, 28th September 2016, https://blog.
politics.ox.ac.uk/1975-referendum-europe, accessed 28th
June 2019.

11   Quoted in Adrian Williamson, 'The case for Brexit:
lessons from the 1960s and 1970s', *History & Policy*,
5th May 2015, http://www.historyandpolicy.org/policy-
papers/papers/the-case-for-brexit-lessons-from-1960s-
and-1970s, accessed 3rd April 2019.

12   Quoted in Christopher Booker, 'Britain and Europe:
The Culture of Deceit', *The Bruges Group*, https://www.
brugesgroup.com/media-centre/papers/8-papers/899-
britain-and-europe-the-culture-of-deceit, accessed 3rd
April 2019.

13   Booker, 'Britain and Europe'.

14   Paul Baldwin, 'We were lied to! Secret document
FCO 30/1048 kept truth about EU from British for 30
years', *Daily Express*, 2nd October 2018, https://www.
express.co.uk/news/politics/882881/Brexit-EU-secret-
document-truth-British-public, accessed 3rd April 2019.

Endnotes

15 Stephen Wall, *A Stranger in Europe* (Oxford University Press, 2008).

16 Quoted in Lars Anell, *Democracy in Europe* (Forum för EU-debatt, 2014).

17 Vernon Bogdanor, 'Why the people should have a vote on Maastricht', *Independent*, 8th June 1993. https://www.independent.co.uk/voices/why-the-people-should-have-a-vote-on-maastricht-the-house-of-lords-must-uphold-democracy-and-insist-1490346.html, accessed 3rd April 2019.

18 David Cameron, 'I'll give EU a vote', *The Sun*, 26th September 2007.

19 David Cameron, 'EU speech at Bloomberg', *Gov.uk*, 23rd January 2017, https://www.gov.uk/government/speeches/eu-speech-at-bloomberg, accessed 3rd April 2019.

20 Robin Niblett, 'Britain, the EU and the Sovereignty Myth', *Chatham House*, 9th May 2016, https://www.chathamhouse.org/publication/britain-eu-and-sovereignty-myth, accessed 3rd April 2019.

21 Vernon Bogdanor, 'The Tories are the party of the nation. No wonder Europe has destroyed so many of its leaders', *The Telegraph*, 29th March 2019, https://www.telegraph.co.uk/politics/2019/03/29/tories-party-nation-no-wonder-brexit-has-toxic-prime-ministers, accessed 28th June 2019.

22 Dominic Cummings, 'How the Brexit referendum was won', *The Spectator*, 9th January 2017, https://blogs.spectator.co.uk/2017/01/dominic-cummings-brexit-referendum-won, accessed 3rd April 2019.

91

23   'Article 50 of the Treaty on European Union',
       UK Parliament, 4th May 2016, https://
       publications.parliament.uk/pa/ld201516/ldselect/
       ldeucom/138/13813.htm, accessed 3rd April 2019.

24   Quoted in Andrew Gray, 'Article 50 author Lord Kerr:
       I didn't have UK in mind', *Politico*, 28th March 2017,
       https://www.politico.eu/article/brexit-article-50-lord-
       kerr-john-kerr, accessed 3rd April 2019.

25   Quoted in Gray, 'Article 50 author Lord Kerr'.

26   Daniel Hannan, *Why Vote Leave* (Head of Zeus, 2016).

27   Hannan, *Why Vote Leave*.

28   'Withdrawal Agreement and Political Declaration',
       Gov.uk, 25th November 2018, https://www.gov.uk/
       government/publications/withdrawal-agreement-and-
       political-declaration, accessed 3rd April 2019.

29   'Withdrawal Agreement and Political Declaration',
       Gov.uk.

30   'Donald Tusk: Special place in hell for Brexiteers
       without a plan', *BBC*, 6th February 2019, https://www.
       bbc.co.uk/news/uk-politics-47143135, accessed 3rd April
       2019.

31   Heather Stewart, 'Brexit could spark democratic
       liberation of continent, says Gove', *The Guardian*,
       19th April 2016, https://www.theguardian.com/
       politics/2016/apr/19/brexit-could-spark-democratic-
       liberation-of-continent-says-gove, accessed 3rd April
       2019.

32   John McCormick, *Why Europe Matters* (Palgrave
       Macmillan, 2013).

33   McCormick, *Why Europe Matters*.

34   *The Conservative Campaign Guide* (Conservative Party, 1979).

35   *European Parliament: Facts and Figures* (European Parliamentary Research Service, April 2018).

36   *Consolidated Texts of the EU Treaties as Amended by the Treaty of Lisbon* (HMSO, 2008), Article 14.

37   Sheila Pulham, 'What exactly does the report say?', *The Guardian*, 16th March 1999, https://www.theguardian.com/world/1999/mar/16/eu.politics, accessed 3rd April 2019.

38   *European Parliament: Facts and Figures* (European Parliamentary Research Service, April 2019).

39   *European Parliament: Facts and Figures* (April 2019).

40   *The power of the European Parliament: Examples of EP impact during the 2014–2019 legislative term* (European Parliamentary Research Service, April 2019).

41   Lord Carrington, *Reflect on Things Past* (Collins, 1988).

42   Michael Heseltine, *The Democratic Deficit* (Centre for Policy Studies, 1989), p. 9.

43   Heseltine, *The Democratic Deficit*, p. 14.

44   Heseltine, *The Democratic Deficit*, p. 23.

45   Heseltine, *The Democratic Deficit*, p. 23.

46   Heseltine, *The Democratic Deficit*, p. 26.

47   Heseltine, *The Democratic Deficit*.

48   Note that ESPAS and ORBIS were created by European Parliament budget amendments originally submitted in my name, not by European Council decisions proposed by member states.

49 ESPAS, *Global Trends 2030: Citizens in an interconnected and polycentric world* (Institute for Security Studies, 2012).

50 ESPAS, *Global Trends to 2030: Can the EU meet the challenges ahead?* (Publications Office of the European Union, 2015).

51 ESPAS, *Global Trends to 2030: Can the EU meet the challenges ahead?*.

52 ESPAS, *Global Trends to 2030: Challenges and Choices for Europe* (European Strategy and Policy Analysis System, 2019).

53 ESPAS, *Global Trends to 2030: Challenges and Choices for Europe.*

54 Kishore Mahbubani, *Has the West Lost It?* (Penguin, 2018), p. 25.

55 John Pomfret, 'A deeper tech concern is at the core of the U.S.-Huawei spat', *Washington Post*, 4th February 2019, https://www.washingtonpost.com/opinions/2019/02/04/deeper-tech-concern-is-core-ushuawei-spat/?utm_term=.b221576e3134.

56 'China's Digital Rise: Challenges for Europe', *Mercator Institute for China Studies*, 8th April 2019, https://www.merics.org/en/papers-on-china/chinas-digital-rise, accessed 1st July 2019.

57 Parag Khanna, *Connectography* (Random House, 2018).

58 Didi Tang, David Charter and Boer Deng, 'Taiwan will be China's by 2050, threatens Xi', *The Times*, 3rd January 2019, https://www.thetimes.co.uk/article/taiwan-will-be-china-s-by-2050-threatens-xi-zqgd59mwm, accessed 3rd April 2019.

59 'Digital change', *Ideas Network 2030*,
http://ideasnetwork2030.com/forum-
digital/#DigitalSummary, accessed 2nd July 2019.

60 'Shoigu: Information becomes another armed forces
component', *Interfax*, 28th March 2015, http://www.
interfax.com/newsinf.asp?id=581851, accessed 3rd April
2019.

61 'Globalisation has faltered', *The Economist*, 26th January
2019.

62 'Globalisation has faltered', *The Economist*.

63 Ulrich Speck, 'Merkel's Defense of the Liberal
Order', *The German Marshall Fund of the United
States*, 19th February 2019, http://www.gmfus.org/
blog/2019/02/19/merkels-defense-liberal-order,
accessed 3rd April 2019.

64 'In Brussels, Menendez Calls for Stronger
U.S.-European Alliance and Support for NATO
in Keynote Speech at German Marshall Fund', *Bob
Menendez for New Jersey*, 18th February 2019, https://
www.menendez.senate.gov/news-and-events/press/
in-brussels-menendez-calls-for-stronger-us-european-
alliance-and-support-for-nato-in-keynote-speech-at-
german-marshall-fund, accessed 3rd April 2019.

65 Quoted in James Kynge, 'China, America and the road
to a new world order', *Financial Times*, 6th December
2018, https://www.ft.com/content/452df746-f880-
11e8-af46-2022a0b02a6c, accessed 2nd April 2019.

66 'Speech by Emmanuel Macron, President of
the Republic at European Parliament', *Élysée*,
17th April 2018, https://www.elysee.fr/

emmanuel-macron/2018/04/17/speech-by-emmanuel-macron-president-of-the-republic-at-european-parliament.en, accessed 1st July 2019.

67   *Three Visions, One Direction: Plans for the Future of Europe* (European Political Strategy Centre, 2018).

68   Guy Chazan, 'Macron and Merkel sign Aachen treaty to deepen Franco-German ties', *Financial Times*, 22nd January 2019, https://www.ft.com/content/fecf3854-1e37-11e9-b2f7-97e4dbd3580d, accessed 2nd July 2019.

69   'Emmanuel Macron's 3 ways to renew Europe', *World Economic Forum*, 10th May 2019, https://www.weforum.org/agenda/2019/05/renewing-europe, accessed 1st July 2019.

70   Matthew Goodwin, 'The EU claims to be more popular than ever, but it is being slowly destroyed by populism', 28th October 2018, *The Telegraph*, https://www.telegraph.co.uk/politics/2018/10/28/eu-claims-popular-ever-slowly-destroyed-populism, accessed 2nd July 2019.

71   'Two new books explain the Brexit revolt', *The Economist*, 3rd November 2018, https://www.economist.com/britain/2018/11/03/two-new-books-explain-the-brexit-revolt, accessed 2nd July 2019.

72   Tom Kington, 'Leave the EU? No chance – we want to confront our problems from inside', *The Times*, 26th January 2019, https://www.thetimes.co.uk/article/giuseppe-conte-interview-leave-the-eu-no-chance-we-want-to-confront-our-problems-from-inside-9vlsglkq8, accessed 2nd July 2019.

73   Jacob Funk Kirkegaard, 'European Elections: Barking populists failed to bite', *Peterson Institute for*

International Economics, 29th May 2019, https://www.
piie.com/blogs/realtime-economic-issues-watch/
european-elections-barking-populists-failed-bite,
accessed 2nd July 2019.

74 'Speech by Mario Draghi, President of the European
Central Bank', *European Central Bank*, 26th July 2012,
https://www.ecb.europa.eu/press/key/date/2012/html/
sp120726.en.html, accessed 3rd April 2019.

75 Mehreen Khan and Tim Bradshaw, 'Apple and
Facebook call for EU-style privacy laws in US', *Financial
Times*, 24th October 2018, https://www.ft.com/
content/0ca8466c-d768-11e8-ab8e-6be0dcf18713,
accessed 3rd April 2019.

76 'Tackling Europe's gap in digital and AI', *McKinsey
& Company*, February 2019, https://www.mckinsey.
com/featured-insights/artificial-intelligence/tackling-
europes-gap-in-digital-and-ai, accessed 2nd July 2019.

77 'Franco-German Treaty of Aachen', *France Diplomatie*,
22nd January 2019, https://www.diplomatie.gouv.fr/
en/country-files/germany/france-and-germany/franco-
german-treaty-of-aachen, accessed 2nd April 2019.

78 ESPAS, *Global Trends to 2030: The Future of Work and
Workplaces* (European Strategy and Policy Analysis
System, 2018).

79 Jan Techau, 'How Europe Got Lucky', *Berlin Policy
Journal*, 29th April 2019, https://berlinpolicyjournal.
com/how-europe-got-lucky, accessed 2nd July 2019.

80 *Europe's two trillion euro dividend: Mapping the Cost
of Non-Europe, 2019–24* (European Parliamentary
Research Service, 2019).

81 'Differentiate or bust: Europe's future is multi-speed and multi-tier', *The Economist*, 25th March 2017.

82 'Differentiate or bust', *The Economist*.

83 Clare Foges, 'Brexit will make Europe stronger than ever', *The Times*, 17th December 2018, https://www.thetimes.co.uk/article/brexit-will-make-europe-stronger-than-ever-5w6gb328d, accessed 2nd April 2019.

84 Andrew Sparrow, 'All at sea: Raab's ignorance of Dover-Calais stuns critics', 8th November 2018, https://www.theguardian.com/politics/2018/nov/08/dominic-raab-dover-calais-brexit-uk-france, accessed 1st August 2019.

85 Hannan, *Why Vote Leave*.

86 Boris Johnson, 'We must be ready to leave the EU if we don't get what we want', *The Telegraph*, 12th May 2013, https://www.telegraph.co.uk/news/politics/10052775/We-must-be-ready-to-leave-the-EU-if-we-dont-get-what-we-want.html, accessed 2nd April 2019.

87 *Flexcit: The Market Solution to leaving the EU* (The Leave Alliance, 2016).

88 Quentin Peel, 'Merkel won't be rushing to rescue May on Brexit', *InFacts*, 29th October 2018, https://infacts.org/merkel-wont-be-rushing-to-rescue-may-on-brexit, accessed 3rd April 2019.

89 Vicky Spratt, 'The truth about young people and Brexit', *BBC*, 5th October 2018, https://www.bbc.co.uk/bbcthree/article/b8d097b0-3ad4-4dd9-aa25-af6374292de0, accessed 3rd April 2019.

90 Stephen Green, *Brexit and the British: Who Are We Now?* (Haus Publishing, 2017).

91   'Risk to business of a no-deal exit from EU', *The Times*, 14th June 2019, https://www.thetimes.co.uk/article/risk-to-business-of-a-no-deal-exit-from-eu-6q57b3jkb, accessed 3rd July 2019.

92   Christopher Booker, 'I knew Brexit would be a shambles, but I never could have predicted this mess', *The Telegraph*, 3rd March 2019, https://www.telegraph.co.uk/politics/2019/03/03/knew-brexit-would-shambles-never-could-have-predicted-mess, accessed 3rd July 2019.

93   'The Times view on Boris Johnson's no-deal Brexit: Eyes Wide Shut', *The Times*, 26th June 2019, https://www.thetimes.co.uk/article/the-times-view-on-boris-johnson-s-no-deal-brexit-eyes-wide-shut-hbxxrro7r, accessed 2nd July 2019.

94   Ivan Rogers, 'The nine Lessons of Brexit', *The Spectator*, 15th December 2018, https://blogs.spectator.co.uk/2018/12/the-nine-lessons-of-brexit, accessed 2nd July 2019.

95   Hannan, *Why Vote Leave*.

96   Peter Oborne, 'I was a strong Brexiteer. Now we must swallow our pride and think again', *openDemocracy*, 7th April 2019, https://www.opendemocracy.net/en/opendemocracyuk/i-was-strong-brexiteer-now-we-must-swallow-our-pride-and-think-again, accessed 3rd July 2019.

97   Ian Goldin and Chris Kutarna, *Age of discovery: Navigating the Risks and Rewards of Our New Renaissance* (Bloomsbury Information, 2016).

HAUS CURIOSITIES

Inspired by the topical pamphlets of the interwar years, as well as by Einstein's advice to 'never lose a holy curiosity', the series presents short works of opinion and analysis by notable figures. Under the guidance of the series editor, Peter Hennessy, Haus Curiosities have been published since 2014.

Welcoming contributions from a diverse pool of authors, the series aims to reinstate the concise and incisive booklet as a powerful strand of politico-literary life, amplifying the voices of those who have something urgent to say about a topical theme.

'Nifty little essays – the thinking person's commuting read'
– *The Independent*

ALSO IN THIS SERIES

The European Identity:
Historical and Cultural Realities We Cannot Deny
by Stephen Green

Breaking Point: The UK Referendum on the EU and its Aftermath
by Gary Gibbon

Brexit and the British: Who Are We Now?
by Stephen Green

These Islands: A Letter to Britain
by Ali M. Ansari

Lion and Lamb: A Portrait of British Moral Duality
By Mihir Bose

The Power of Politicians
by Tessa Jowell and Frances D'Souza

The Power of Civil Servants
by David Normington and Peter Hennessy

The Power of Judges
by David Neuberger and Peter Riddell

The Power of Journalists
by Nick Robinson, Barbara Speed, Charlie Beckett and Gary Gibbon

Drawing the Line: The Irish Border in British Politics
by Ivan Gibbons

Not for Patching: A Strategic Welfare Review
by Frank Field and Andrew Forsey

A Love Affair with Europe: The Case for a European Future
by Giles Radice